FOREWORD

The collection of "Everything Will Be Okay" travel phrasebooks published by T&P Books is designed for people traveling abroad for tourism and business. The phrasebooks contain what matters most - the essentials for basic communication. This is an indispensable set of phrases to "survive" while abroad.

This phrasebook will help you in most cases where you need to ask something, get directions, find out how much something costs, etc. It can also resolve difficult communication situations where gestures just won't help.

This book contains a lot of phrases that have been grouped according to the most relevant topics. The edition also includes a small vocabulary that contains roughly 3,000 of the most frequently used words. Another section of the phrasebook provides a gastronomical dictionary that may help you order food at a restaurant or buy groceries at the store.

Take "Everything Will Be Okay" phrasebook with you on the road and you'll have an irreplaceable traveling companion who will help you find your way out of any situation and teach you to not fear speaking with foreigners.

TABLE OF CONTENTS

T&P Books Publishing

T&P Books Publishing

PHRASEBOOK
- JAPANESE -

By Andrey Taranov

THE MOST IMPORTANT PHRASES

This phrasebook contains
the most important
phrases and questions
for basic communication
Everything you need
to survive overseas

T&P BOOKS

Phrasebook + 3000-word dictionary

English-Japanese phrasebook & topical vocabulary

By Andrey Taranov

The collection of "Everything Will Be Okay" travel phrasebooks published by T&P Books is designed for people traveling abroad for tourism and business. The phrasebooks contain what matters most - the essentials for basic communication. This is an indispensable set of phrases to "survive" while abroad.

This book also includes a small topical vocabulary that contains roughly 3,000 of the most frequently used words. Another section of the phrasebook provides a gastronomical dictionary that may help you order food at a restaurant or buy groceries at the store.

T&P Books Publishing
www.tpbooks.com

ISBN: 978-1-78492-427-0

This book is also available in E-book formats.
Please visit www.tpbooks.com or the major online bookstores.

PRONUNCIATION

Hiragana	Katakana	Rōmaji	Japanese example	T&P phonetic alphabet	English example

Consonants

Hiragana	Katakana	Rōmaji	Japanese example	T&P phonetic alphabet	English example
あ	ア	a	あなた	[a]	shorter than in ask
い	イ	i	いす	[i], [iː]	feet, Peter
う	ウ	u	うた	[u], [uː]	book, shoe
え	エ	e	いいえ	[e]	elm, medal
お	オ	o	しお	[ɔ]	bottle, doctor
や	ヤ	ya	やすみ	[jɑ]	young, yard
ゆ	ユ	yu	ふゆ	[ju]	youth, usually
よ	ヨ	yo	ようす	[jɔ]	New York

Syllables

Hiragana	Katakana	Rōmaji	Japanese example	T&P phonetic alphabet	English example
ば	バ	b	ばん	[b]	baby, book
ち	チ	ch	ちち	[tʃ]	cheese
だ	ダ	d	からだ	[d]	day, doctor
ふ	フ	f	ひふ	[f]	face, food
が	ガ	g	がっこう	[g]	game, gold
は	ハ	h	はは	[h]	home, have
じ	ジ	j	じしょ	[dʒ]	joke, general
か	カ	k	かぎ	[k]	clock, kiss
む	ム	m	さむらい	[m]	magic, milk
に	ニ	n	にもつ	[n]	name, normal
ぱ	パ	p	パン	[p]	pencil, private
ら	ラ	r	いくら	[r]	rice, radio
さ	サ	s	あさ	[s]	city, boss
し	シ	sh	わたし	[ɕ]	sheep, shop
た	タ	t	ふた	[t]	tourist, trip
つ	ツ	ts	いくつ	[ts]	cats, tsetse fly
わ	ワ	w	わた	[w]	vase, winter
ざ	ザ	z	ざっし	[dz]	beads, kids

LIST OF ABBREVIATIONS

English abbreviations

ab.	-	about
adj	-	adjective
adv	-	adverb
anim.	-	animate
as adj	-	attributive noun used as adjective
e.g.	-	for example
etc.	-	et cetera
fam.	-	familiar
fem.	-	feminine
form.	-	formal
inanim.	-	inanimate
masc.	-	masculine
math	-	mathematics
mil.	-	military
n	-	noun
pl	-	plural
pron.	-	pronoun
sb	-	somebody
sing.	-	singular
sth	-	something
v aux	-	auxiliary verb
vi	-	intransitive verb
vi, vt	-	intransitive, transitive verb
vt	-	transitive verb

T&P BOOKS

JAPANESE PHRASEBOOK

This section contains
important phrases that may
come in handy in various
real-life situations.
The phrasebook will help
you ask for directions, clarify
a price, buy tickets, and
order food at a restaurant

T&P Books Publishing

PHRASEBOOK
CONTENTS

T&P Books Publishing

The bare minimum

Excuse me, ...
すみません、…
[sumimasen, …]

Hello.
こんにちは。
[konnichiwa]

Thank you.
ありがとうございます。
[arigatō gozai masu]

Good bye.
さようなら。
[sayōnara]

Yes.
はい。
[hai]

No.
いいえ。
[īe]

I don't know.
わかりません。
[wakari masen]

Where? | Where to? | When?
どこ？ | どこへ？ | いつ？
[doko ? | doko e ? | i tsu ?]

I need ...
…が必要です
[… ga hitsuyō desu]

I want ...
したいです
[shi tai desu]

Do you have ...?
…をお持ちですか？
[… wo o mochi desu ka ?]

Is there a ... here?
ここには…がありますか？
[koko ni wa … ga ari masu ka ?]

May I ...?
…してもいいですか？
[… shi te mo ī desu ka ?]

..., please (polite request)
お願いします。
[onegai shi masu]

I'm looking for ...
…を探しています
[… wo sagashi te i masu]

restroom
トイレ
[toire]

ATM
ＡＴＭ
[ētīemu]

pharmacy (drugstore)
薬局
[yakkyoku]

hospital
病院
[byōin]

police station
警察
[keisatsu]

subway
地下鉄
[chikatetsu]

taxi	タクシー [takushī]
train station	駅 [eki]

My name is …	私は…と申します [watashi wa … to mōshi masu]
What's your name?	お名前は何ですか？ [o namae wa nan desu ka ?]
Could you please help me?	助けていただけますか？ [tasuke te itadake masu ka ?]
I've got a problem.	困ったことがあります。 [komatta koto ga arimasu]
I don't feel well.	気分が悪いのです。 [kibun ga warui nodesu]
Call an ambulance!	救急車を呼んで下さい！ [kyūkyū sha wo yon de kudasai !]
May I make a call?	電話をしてもいいですか？ [denwa wo shi te mo ī desu ka ?]

I'm sorry.	ごめんなさい。 [gomennasai]
You're welcome.	どういたしまして。 [dōitashimashite]

I, me	私 [watashi]
you (inform.)	君 [kimi]
he	彼 [kare]
she	彼女 [kanojo]
they (masc.)	彼ら [karera]
they (fem.)	彼女たち [kanojotachi]
we	私たち [watashi tachi]
you (pl)	君たち [kimi tachi]
you (sg, form.)	あなた [anata]

ENTRANCE	入り口 [iriguchi]
EXIT	出口 [deguchi]
OUT OF ORDER	故障中 [koshō chū]
CLOSED	休業中 [kyūgyō chū]

OPEN	営業中
	[eigyō chū]
FOR WOMEN	女性用
	[josei yō]
FOR MEN	男性用
	[dansei yō]

Questions

Where?	どこ？ [doko ?]
Where to?	どこへ？ [doko e ?]
Where from?	どこから？ [doko kara ?]
Why?	どうしてですか？ [dōshite desu ka ?]
For what reason?	なんのためですか？ [nan no tame desu ka ?]
When?	いつですか？ [i tsu desu ka ?]
How long?	どのぐらいですか？ [dono gurai desu ka ?]
At what time?	何時にですか？ [nan ji ni desu ka ?]
How much?	いくらですか？ [ikura desu ka ?]
Do you have ...?	…をお持ちですか？ [... wo o mochi desu ka ?]
Where is ...?	…はどこですか？ [... wa doko desu ka ?]
What time is it?	何時ですか？ [nan ji desu ka ?]
May I make a call?	電話をしてもいいですか？ [denwa wo shi te mo ī desu ka ?]
Who's there?	誰ですか？ [dare desu ka ?]
Can I smoke here?	ここでタバコを吸ってもいいですか？ [koko de tabako wo sutte mo ī desu ka ?]
May I ...?	…してもいいですか？ [... shi te mo ī desu ka ?]

Needs

I'd like ...

…をしたいのですが
[... wo shi tai no desu ga]

I don't want ...

…したくないです
[... shi taku nai desu]

I'm thirsty.

喉が渇きました。
[nodo ga kawaki mashi ta]

I want to sleep.

眠りたいです。
[nemuri tai desu]

I want ...

したいです
[shi tai desu]

to wash up

洗いたい
[arai tai]

to brush my teeth

歯を磨きたい
[ha wo migaki tai]

to rest a while

しばらく休みたい
[shibaraku yasumi tai]

to change my clothes

着替えたい
[kigae tai]

to go back to the hotel

ホテルに戻る
[hoteru ni modoru]

to buy ...

…を買う
[... wo kau]

to go to ...

…へ行く
[... e iku]

to visit ...

…を訪問する
[... wo hōmon suru]

to meet with ...

…と会う
[... to au]

to make a call

電話をする
[denwa wo suru]

I'm tired.

疲れています。
[tsukare te i masu]

We are tired.

私たちは疲れました。
[watashi tachi wa tsukare mashita]

I'm cold.

寒いです。
[samui desu]

I'm hot.

暑いです。
[atsui desu]

I'm OK.

大丈夫です。
[daijōbu desu]

I need to make a call.

電話をしなければなりません。
[denwa wo shi nakere ba nari masen]

I need to go to the restroom.

トイレへ行きたいです。
[toire e iki tai desu]

I have to go.

行かなければいけません。
[ika nakere ba ike masen]

I have to go now.

今すぐ行かなければいけません。
[ima sugu ika nakere ba ike masen]

Asking for directions

Excuse me, ...	すみません、… [sumimasen, ...]
Where is ...?	…はどこですか？ [... wa doko desu ka ?]
Which way is ...?	…はどちらですか？ [...wa dochira desu ka ?]
Could you help me, please?	助けていただけますか？ [tasuke te itadake masu ka ?]
I'm looking for ...	…を探しています [... wo sagashi te i masu]
I'm looking for the exit.	出口を探しています。 [deguchi wo sagashi te i masu]
I'm going to ...	…へ行く予定です [... e iku yotei desu]
Am I going the right way to ...?	…へはこの道で合っていますか？ [...e wa kono michi de atte i masu ka ?]
Is it far?	遠いですか？ [tōi desu ka ?]
Can I get there on foot?	そこまで歩いて行けますか？ [soko made arui te ike masu ka ?]
Can you show me on the map?	地図で教えて頂けますか？ [chizu de oshie te itadake masu ka ?]
Show me where we are right now.	今どこにいるかを教えて下さい。 [ima doko ni iru ka wo oshie te kudasai]
Here	ここです [koko desu]
There	あちらです [achira desu]
This way	こちらです [kochira desu]
Turn right.	右に曲がって下さい。 [migi ni magatte kudasai]
Turn left.	左に曲がって下さい。 [hidari ni magatte kudasai]
first (second, third) turn	1つ目（2つ目、3つ目） の曲がり角 [hitotsume (futatsume, mittsume) no magarikado]
to the right	右に [migi ni]

to the left

左に
[hidari ni]

Go straight.

まっすぐ歩いて下さい。
[massugu arui te kudasai]

Signs

WELCOME!	いらっしゃいませ！ [irasshai mase !]
ENTRANCE	入り口 [iriguchi]
EXIT	出口 [deguchi]

PUSH	押す [osu]
PULL	引く [hiku]
OPEN	営業中 [eigyō chū]
CLOSED	休業中 [kyūgyō chū]

FOR WOMEN	女性用 [josei yō]
FOR MEN	男性用 [dansei yō]
MEN, GENTS	男性用 [dansei yō]
WOMEN, LADIES	女性用 [josei yō]

DISCOUNTS	営業 [eigyō]
SALE	セール [sēru]
FREE	無料 [muryō]
NEW!	新商品！ [shin shōhin !]
ATTENTION!	目玉品！ [medama hin !]

NO VACANCIES	満員 [man in]
RESERVED	ご予約済み [go yoyaku zumi]
ADMINISTRATION	管理 [kanri]
STAFF ONLY	社員専用 [shain senyō]

BEWARE OF THE DOG!   猛犬注意
                           [mōken chūi]

NO SMOKING!   禁煙！
                           [kin en !]

DO NOT TOUCH!   触るな危険！
                           [sawaru na kiken !]

DANGEROUS   危ない
                           [abunai]

DANGER   危険
                           [kiken]

HIGH VOLTAGE   高電圧
                           [kō denatsu]

NO SWIMMING!   水泳禁止！
                           [suiei kinshi !]

OUT OF ORDER   故障中
                           [koshō chū]

FLAMMABLE   火気注意
                           [kaki chūi]

FORBIDDEN   禁止
                           [kinshi]

NO TRESPASSING!   通り抜け禁止！
                           [tōrinuke kinshi !]

WET PAINT   ペンキ塗り立て
                           [penki nuritate]

CLOSED FOR RENOVATIONS   改装閉鎖中
                           [kaisō heisa chū]

WORKS AHEAD   この先工事中
                           [kono saki kōji chū]

DETOUR   迂回
                           [ukai]

Transportation. General phrases

plane	飛行機 [hikōki]
train	電車 [densha]
bus	バス [basu]
ferry	フェリー [ferī]
taxi	タクシー [takushī]
car	車 [kuruma]

schedule	時刻表 [jikoku hyō]
Where can I see the schedule?	どこで時刻表を見られますか？ [doko de jikoku hyō wo mirare masu ka ?]
workdays (weekdays)	平日 [heijitsu]
weekends	週末 [shūmatsu]
holidays	祝日 [kokumin no syukujitsu]

DEPARTURE	出発 [shuppatsu]
ARRIVAL	到着 [tōchaku]
DELAYED	遅延 [chien]
CANCELED	欠航 [kekkō]

next (train, etc.)	次の [tsugi no]
first	最初の [saisho no]
last	最後の [saigono]

When is the next ...?	次の…はいつですか？ [tsugi no ... wa i tsu desu ka ?]
When is the first ...?	最初の…はいつですか？ [saisho no ... wa i tsu desu ka ?]

When is the last ...?

最後の…はいつですか？
[saigo no ... wa i tsu desu ka ?]

transfer (change of trains, etc.)

乗り継ぎ
[noritsugi]

to make a transfer

乗り継ぎをする
[noritsugi wo suru]

Do I need to make a transfer?

乗り継ぎをする必要がありますか？
[noritsugi o suru hitsuyō ga ari masu ka ?]

Buying tickets

Where can I buy tickets?	どこで乗車券を買えますか？ [doko de jōsha ken wo kae masu ka ?]
ticket	乗車券 [jōsha ken]
to buy a ticket	乗車券を買う [jōsha ken wo kau]
ticket price	乗車券の値段 [jōsha ken no nedan]
Where to?	どこへ？ [doko e ?]
To what station?	どこの駅へ？ [doko no eki e ?]
I need ...	…が必要です [... ga hitsuyō desu]
one ticket	券 1枚 [ken ichi mai]
two tickets	2枚 [ni mai]
three tickets	3枚 [san mai]
one-way	片道 [katamichi]
round-trip	往復 [ōfuku]
first class	ファーストクラス [fāsuto kurasu]
second class	エコノミークラス [ekonomī kurasu]
today	今日 [kyō]
tomorrow	明日 [ashita]
the day after tomorrow	あさって [asatte]
in the morning	朝に [asa ni]
in the afternoon	昼に [hiru ni]
in the evening	晩に [ban ni]

aisle seat

通路側の席
[tsūro gawa no seki]

window seat

窓側の席
[madogawa no seki]

How much?

いくらですか？
[ikura desu ka ?]

Can I pay by credit card?

カードで支払いができますか？
[kādo de shiharai ga deki masu ka ?]

Bus

bus	バス [basu]
intercity bus	高速バス [kōsoku basu]
bus stop	バス停 [basutei]
Where's the nearest bus stop?	最寄りのバス停はどこですか？ [moyori no basutei wa doko desu ka ?]
number (bus ~, etc.)	数 [kazu]
Which bus do I take to get to ...?	…に行くにはどのバスに乗れば いいですか ？ [...ni iku niwa dono basu ni nore ba ī desu ka ...?]
Does this bus go to ...?	このバスは…まで行きますか？ [kono basu wa ... made iki masu ka ?]
How frequent are the buses?	バスはどのくらいの頻度で 来ますか？ [basu wa dono kurai no hindo de ki masu ka?]
every 15 minutes	１５分おき [jyū go fun oki]
every half hour	３０分おき [sanjuppun oki]
every hour	１時間に　１回 [ichi jikan ni ittu kai]
several times a day	１日に数回 [ichi nichi ni sū kai]
... times a day	１日に…回 [ichi nichi ni ... kai]
schedule	時刻表 [jikoku hyō]
Where can I see the schedule?	どこで時刻表を見られますか？ [doko de jikoku hyō wo mirare masu ka ?]
When is the next bus?	次のバスは何時ですか？ [tsugi no basu wa nan ji desu ka ?]
When is the first bus?	最初のバスは何時ですか？ [saisho no basu wa nan ji desu ka ?]
When is the last bus?	最後のバスは何時ですか？ [saigo no basu wa nan ji desu ka ?]

stop	バス停、停留所
	[basutei, teiryūjo]
next stop	次のバス停、次の停留所
	[tsugi no basutei, tsugi no teiryūjo]
last stop (terminus)	最終停留所
	[saishū teiryūjo]
Stop here, please.	ここで止めてください。
	[koko de tome te kudasai]
Excuse me, this is my stop.	すみません、ここで降ります。
	[sumimasen, koko de ori masu]

Train

train
電車
[densha]

suburban train
郊外電車
[kōgai densha]

long-distance train
長距離列車
[chōkyori ressha]

train station
電車の駅
[densha no eki]

Excuse me, where is the exit
to the platform?
すみません、ホームへはど
う行けばいいですか？
[sumimasen, hōmu e wa dō
ike ba ī desu ka?]

Does this train go to ...?
この電車は…まで行きますか？
[kono densha wa ... made iki masu ka ?]

next train
次の駅
[tsugi no eki]

When is the next train?
次の電車は何時ですか？
[tsugi no densha wa nan ji desu ka ?]

Where can I see the schedule?
どこで時刻表を見られますか？
[doko de jikoku hyō wo mirare masu ka ?]

From which platform?
どのホームからですか？
[dono hōmu kara desu ka ?]

When does the train arrive in ...?
電車はいつ到着しますか…？
[densha wa i tsu tōchaku
shi masu ka ...?]

Please help me.
助けて下さい。
[tasuke te kudasai]

I'm looking for my seat.
私の座席を探しています。
[watashi no zaseki wo sagashi te i masu]

We're looking for our seats.
私たちの座席を探し
ています。
[watashi tachi no zaseki wo sagashi
te i masu]

My seat is taken.
私の席に他の人が
座っています。
[watashi no seki ni hoka no hito ga
suwatte i masu]

Our seats are taken.
私たちの席に他の人が
座っています。
[watashi tachi no seki ni hoka no hito ga
suwatte i masu.]

I'm sorry but this is my seat.

すみませんが、こちらは私
の席です。
[sumimasen ga, kochira wa watashi
no seki desu]

Is this seat taken?

この席はふさがっていますか？
[kono seki wa husagatte i masu ka ?]

May I sit here?

ここに座ってもいいですか？
[koko ni suwatte mo ī desu ka ?]

On the train. Dialogue (No ticket)

Ticket, please.	乗車券を見せて下さい。 [jōsha ken wo mise te kudasai]
I don't have a ticket.	乗車券を持っていません。 [jōsha ken wo motte i masen]
I lost my ticket.	乗車券を失くしました。 [jōsha ken wo nakushi mashi ta]
I forgot my ticket at home.	乗車券を家に忘れました。 [jōsha ken wo ie ni wasure mashi ta]
You can buy a ticket from me.	私からも乗車券を購入できます。 [watashi kara mo jōsha ken wo kōnyū deki masu]
You will also have to pay a fine.	それから罰金を払わなければいけません。 [sorekara bakkin wo harawa nakere ba ike masen]
Okay.	わかりました。 [wakari mashi ta]
Where are you going?	行き先はどこですか？ [yukisaki wa doko desu ka ?]
I'm going to …	…に行きます。 [… ni iki masu]
How much? I don't understand.	いくらですか？ わかりません。 [ikura desu ka ? wakari masen]
Write it down, please.	書いてください。 [kai te kudasai]
Okay. Can I pay with a credit card?	わかりました。クレジットカードで支払いできますか？ [wakari mashi ta. kurejittokādo de shiharaideki masu ka?]
Yes, you can.	はい。 [hai]
Here's your receipt.	レシートです。 [reshīto desu]
Sorry about the fine.	罰金をいただいてすみません。 [bakkin wo itadaite sumimasen]
That's okay. It was my fault.	大丈夫です。私のせいですから。 [daijōbu desu. watashi no sei desu kara]
Enjoy your trip.	良い旅を。 [yoi tabi wo]

Taxi

taxi	タクシー [takushī]
taxi driver	タクシー運転手 [takushī unten shu]
to catch a taxi	タクシーをひろう [takushī wo hirō]
taxi stand	タクシー乗り場 [takushī noriba]
Where can I get a taxi?	どこでタクシーをひろえますか？ [doko de takushī wo hiroe masu ka ?]
to call a taxi	タクシーを呼ぶ [takushī wo yobu]
I need a taxi.	タクシーが必要です。 [takushī ga hitsuyō desu]
Right now.	今すぐ。 [ima sugu]
What is your address (location)?	住所はどこですか？ [jūsho wa doko desu ka ?]
My address is ...	私の住所は…です [watashi no jūsho wa ... desu]
Your destination?	どちらへ行かれますか？ [dochira e ikare masu ka ?]
Excuse me, ...	すみません、… [sumimasen, ...]
Are you available?	乗ってもいいですか？ [nottemo ī desu ka ?]
How much is it to get to ...?	…までいくらですか？ [... made ikura desu ka ?]
Do you know where it is?	どこにあるかご存知ですか？ [doko ni aru ka gozonji desu ka ?]
Airport, please.	空港へお願いします。 [kūkō e onegai shi masu]
Stop here, please.	ここで止めてください。 [koko de tome te kudasai]
It's not here.	ここではありません。 [koko de wa ari masen]
This is the wrong address.	その住所は間違っています。 [sono jūsho wa machigatte i masu]
Turn left.	左へ曲がって下さい [hidari e magatte kudasai]
Turn right.	右へ曲がって下さい [migi e magatte kudasai]

How much do I owe you?	いくらですか？ [ikura desu ka ?]
I'd like a receipt, please.	領収書を下さい。 [ryōshū sho wo kudasai]
Keep the change.	おつりはいりません。 [o tsuri hairi masen]

Would you please wait for me?	待っていて頂けますか？ [matte i te itadake masu ka?]
five minutes	5分 [go fun]
ten minutes	10分 [juppun]
fifteen minutes	15分 [jyū go fun]
twenty minutes	20分 [nijuppun]
half an hour	30分 [sanjuppun]

Hotel

Hello.	こんにちは。 [konnichiwa]
My name is ...	私の名前は…です [watashi no namae wa ... desu]
I have a reservation.	予約をしました。 [yoyaku wo shi mashi ta]

I need ...	私は…が必要です [watashi wa ... ga hitsuyō desu]
a single room	シングルルーム [shinguru rūmu]
a double room	ツインルーム [tsuin rūmu]
How much is that?	いくらですか？ [ikura desu ka ?]
That's a bit expensive.	それは少し高いです。 [sore wa sukoshi takai desu]

Do you have any other options?	他にも選択肢はありますか？ [hoka ni mo sentakushi wa ari masu ka ?]
I'll take it.	それにします。 [sore ni shi masu]
I'll pay in cash.	現金で払います。 [genkin de harai masu]

I've got a problem.	困ったことがあります。 [komatta koto ga arimasu]
My ... is broken.	私の…が壊れています。 [watashi no ... ga koware te i masu]
My ... is out of order.	私の…が故障しています。 [watashi no ... ga koshō shi te i masu]
TV	テレビ [terebi]
air conditioning	エアコン [eakon]
tap	蛇口 [jaguchi]

shower	シャワー [shawā]
sink	流し台 [nagashi dai]
safe	金庫 [kinko]

door lock	錠 [jō]
electrical outlet	電気のコンセント [dengen no konsento]
hairdryer	ドライヤー [doraiyā]

I don't have ...	…がありません [… ga ari masen]
water	水 [mizu]
light	明かり [akari]
electricity	電気 [denki]

Can you give me ...?	…を頂けませんか？ [… wo itadake masenka ?]
a towel	タオル [taoru]
a blanket	毛布 [mōfu]
slippers	スリッパ [surippa]
a robe	バスローブ [basurōbu]
shampoo	シャンプーを何本か [shanpū wo nannbon ka]
soap	石鹸をいくつか [sekken wo ikutsu ka]

I'd like to change rooms.	部屋を変えたいのですが。 [heya wo kae tai no desu ga]
I can't find my key.	鍵が見つかりません。 [kagi ga mitsukarimasenn]
Could you open my room, please?	部屋を開けて頂けますか？ [heya wo ake te itadake masu ka ?]
Who's there?	誰ですか？ [dare desu ka ?]
Come in!	どうぞお入り下さい [dōzo o hairikudasai]
Just a minute!	少々お待ち下さい！ [shōshō omachi kudasai !]
Not right now, please.	後にしてもらえますか。 [ato ni shi te morae masu ka]

Come to my room, please.	私の部屋に来て下さい。 [watashi no heya ni ki te kudasai]
I'd like to order food service.	食事サービスをお願いしたい のですが。 [shokuji sābisu wo onegai shi tai no desu ga]

My room number is …
私の部屋の番号は…
[watashi no heya no bangō wa …]

I'm leaving …
チェックアウトします…
[tyekkuauto shi masu …]

We're leaving …
私たちはチェックアウトします…
[watashi tachi wa tyekkuauto shi masu …]

right now
今すぐ
[ima sugu]

this afternoon
今日の午後
[kyō no gogo]

tonight
今晩
[konban]

tomorrow
明日
[ashita]

tomorrow morning
明日の朝
[ashita no asa]

tomorrow evening
明日の夕方
[ashita no yūgata]

the day after tomorrow
あさって
[asatte]

I'd like to pay.
支払いをしたいのですが。
[shiharai wo shi tai no desu ga]

Everything was wonderful.
何もかもがよかったです。
[nanimokamo ga yokatta desu]

Where can I get a taxi?
どこでタクシーをひろえますか？
[doko de takushī wo hiroe masu ka ?]

Would you call a taxi for me, please?
タクシーを呼んでいただけますか？
[takushī wo yon de itadake masu ka ?]

Restaurant

Can I look at the menu, please?	メニューを頂けますか？ [menyū wo itadake masu ka ?]
Table for one.	一人用の席をお願いします。 [hitori yō no seki wo onegai shimasu]
There are two (three, four) of us.	2人（3人、4人）です。 [futari (san nin, yon nin) desu]

Smoking	喫煙 [kitsuen]
No smoking	禁煙 [kinen]
Excuse me! (addressing a waiter)	すみません！ [sumimasen !]
menu	メニュー [menyū]
wine list	ワインリスト [wain risuto]
The menu, please.	メニューを下さい。 [menyū wo kudasai]

Are you ready to order?	ご注文をお伺いしても よろしいですか？ [go chūmon wo o ukagai shi te mo yoroshī desu ka?]
What will you have?	ご注文は何にしますか？ [go chūmon wa nani ni shi masu ka ?]
I'll have ...	…を下さい。 [… wo kudasai]

I'm a vegetarian.	私はベジタリアンです。 [watashi wa bejitarian desu]
meat	肉 [niku]
fish	魚 [sakana]
vegetables	野菜 [yasai]
Do you have vegetarian dishes?	ベジタリアン向けの料理はありますか？ [bejitarian muke no ryōri wa ari masu ka?]
I don't eat pork.	私は豚肉を食べません。 [watashi wa butaniku o tabe masen]

He /she/ doesn't eat meat. 彼 /彼女/ は肉を食べません。
[kare /kanojo/ wa niku o tabe masen]

I am allergic to … 私は…にアレルギーがあります
[watashi wa … ni arerugī ga ari masu]

Would you please bring me … …を持ってきてもらえますか
[… wo motte ki te morae masu ka]

salt | pepper | sugar 塩 | 胡椒 | 砂糖
[shio | koshō | satō]

coffee | tea | dessert コーヒー | お茶 | デザート
[kōhī | ocha | dezāto]

water | sparkling | plain 水 | スパークリングウォーター | 真水
[mizu | supāku ringu wōtā | mamizu]

a spoon | fork | knife スプーン | フォーク | ナイフ
[supūn | fōku | naifu]

a plate | napkin プレート | ナプキン
[purēto | napukin]

Enjoy your meal! どうぞお召し上がりください
[dōzo omeshiagari kudasai]

One more, please. もう一つお願いします。
[mō hitotsu onegai shi masu]

It was very delicious. とても美味しかったです。
[totemo oishikatta desu]

check | change | tip 勘定 | おつり | チップ
[kanjō | o tsuri | chippu]

Check, please. お勘定をお願いします。
(Could I have the check, please?) [o kanjō wo onegai shi masu]

Can I pay by credit card? カードで支払いができますか？
[kādo de shiharai ga deki masu ka ?]

I'm sorry, there's a mistake here. すみません、間違いがあります。
[sumimasen, machigai ga ari masu]

Shopping

Can I help you?	いらっしゃいませ。 [irasshai mase]
Do you have …?	…をお持ちですか？ [… wo o mochi desu ka ?]
I'm looking for …	…を探しています [… wo sagashi te i masu]
I need …	…が必要です [… ga hitsuyō desu]
I'm just looking.	ただ見ているだけです。 [tada mi te iru dake desu]
We're just looking.	私たちはただ見ているだけです。 [watashi tachi wa tada mi te iru dake desu]
I'll come back later.	また後で来ます。 [mata atode ki masu]
We'll come back later.	また後で来ます。 [mata atode ki masu]
discounts | sale	値引き ｜ セール [nebiki | sēru]
Would you please show me …	…を見せていただけますか [… wo mise te itadake masu ka]
Would you please give me …	…をいただけますか [… wo itadake masu ka]
Can I try it on?	試着できますか？ [shichaku deki masu ka ?]
Excuse me, where's the fitting room?	すみません、試着室は どこですか？ [sumimasen, shichaku shitsu wa doko desu ka?]
Which color would you like?	どの色がお好みですか？ [dono iro ga o konomi desu ka ?]
size | length	サイズ ｜ 長さ [saizu | naga sa]
How does it fit?	サイズは合いましたか？ [saizu wa ai mashi ta ka ?]
How much is it?	これはいくらですか？ [kore wa ikura desu ka ?]
That's too expensive.	高すぎます。 [takasugi masu]

I'll take it.

これにします。
[kore ni shi masu]

Excuse me, where do I pay?

すみません、どこで支払いますか？
[sumimasen, doko de shiharai masu ka ?]

Will you pay in cash or credit card?

現金とクレジットカードのどちら
でお支払いされますか？
[genkin to kurejittokādo no dochira
de o shiharai sare masu ka?]

In cash | with credit card

現金 | クレジットカード
[genkin | kurejittokādo]

Do you want the receipt?

レシートはお入り用ですか？
[reshīto ha oiriyō desu ka ?]

Yes, please.

お願いします。
[onegai shi masu]

No, it's OK.

いえ、結構です。
[ie, kekkō desu]

Thank you. Have a nice day!

ありがとうございます。良い一日を！
[arigatō gozai masu. yoi ichi nichi wo !]

In town

Excuse me, please.	すみません、… [sumimasen, …]
I'm looking for ...	…を探しています [watashi wa ... wo sagashi te i masu]
the subway	地下鉄 [chikatetsu]
my hotel	ホテル [hoteru]
the movie theater	映画館 [eiga kan]
a taxi stand	タクシー乗り場 [takushī noriba]
an ATM	ＡＴＭ [ētīemu]
a foreign exchange office	両替所 [ryōgae sho]
an internet café	インターネットカフェ [intānetto kafe]
... street	…通り [... tōri]
this place	この場所 [kono basho]
Do you know where ... is?	…がどこにあるかご存知ですか？ [... ga doko ni aru ka gozonji desu ka ?]
Which street is this?	この通りの名前は何ですか？ [kono michi no namae wa nani desu ka ?]
Show me where we are right now.	今どこにいるかを教えて下さい。 [ima doko ni iru ka wo oshie te kudasai]
Can I get there on foot?	そこまで歩いて行けますか？ [soko made arui te ike masu ka?]
Do you have a map of the city?	市内地図をお持ちですか？ [shinai chizu wo o mochi desu ka ?]
How much is a ticket to get in?	チケットはいくらですか？ [chiketto wa ikura desu ka ?]
Can I take pictures here?	ここで写真を撮ってもいいですか？ [koko de shashin wo totte mo ī desu ka ?]
Are you open?	開いていますか？ [hirai te i masu ka ?]

When do you open?

何時に開きますか？
[nan ji ni hiraki masu ka ?]

When do you close?

何時に閉まりますか？
[nan ji ni shimari masu ka ?]

Money

money	お金 [okane]
cash	現金 [genkin]
paper money	紙幣 [shihei]
loose change	おつり [o tsuri]
check | change | tip	勘定 ｜ おつり ｜ チップ [kanjō | o tsuri | chippu]
credit card	クレジットカード [kurejittokādo]
wallet	財布 [saifu]
to buy	買う [kau]
to pay	支払う [shiharau]
fine	罰金 [bakkin]
free	無料 [muryō]
Where can I buy …?	…はどこで買えますか？ [… wa doko de kae masu ka ?]
Is the bank open now?	銀行は今開いていますか？ [ginkō wa ima hirai te i masu ka ?]
When does it open?	いつ開きますか？ [itsu hiraki masu ka ?]
When does it close?	いつ閉まりますか？ [itsu shimari masu ka ?]
How much?	いくらですか？ [ikura desu ka ?]
How much is this?	これはいくらですか？ [kore wa ikura desu ka ?]
That's too expensive.	高すぎます。 [takasugi masu]
Excuse me, where do I pay?	すみません、レジはどこですか？ [sumimasen, reji wa doko desu ka ?]
Check, please.	勘定をお願いします。 [kanjō wo onegai shi masu]

Can I pay by credit card? カードで支払いができますか？
[kādo de shiharai ga deki masu ka ?]

Is there an ATM here? ここにＡＴＭはありますか？
[kokoni ētīemu wa ari masu ka ?]

I'm looking for an ATM. ＡＴＭを探しています。
[ētīemu wo sagashi te i masu]

I'm looking for a foreign exchange office. 両替所を探しています。
[ryōgae sho wo sagashi te i masu]

I'd like to change … 両替をしたいのですが…
[ryōgae wo shi tai no desu ga…]

What is the exchange rate? 為替レートはいくらですか？
[kawase rēto wa ikura desu ka ?]

Do you need my passport? パスポートは必要ですか？
[pasupōto ha hituyō desu ka ?]

Time

What time is it?	何時ですか？ [nan ji desu ka ?]
When?	いつですか？ [i tsu desu ka ?]
At what time?	何時にですか？ [nan ji ni desu ka ?]
now | later | after …	今 ｜ 1 後で ｜ …の後 [ima |ato de ｜ … no ato]
one o'clock	1 時 [ichi ji]
one fifteen	1 時 1 5分 [ichi ji jyū go fun]
one thirty	1 時半 [ichi ji han]
one forty-five	1 時4 5分 [ichi ji yon jyū go fun]
one | two | three	1 ｜ 2 ｜ 3 [ichi | ni | san]
four | five | six	4 ｜ 5 ｜ 6 [yonn | go |roku]
seven | eight | nine	7 ｜ 8 ｜ 9 [shichi | hachi | kyū]
ten | eleven | twelve	1 0 ｜ 1 1 ｜ 1 2 [jyū | jyūichi | jyūni]
in …	…後 [… go]
five minutes	5分 [go fun]
ten minutes	1 0分 [juppun]
fifteen minutes	1 5分 [jyū go fun]
twenty minutes	2 0分 [nijuppun]
half an hour	3 0分 [sanjuppun]
an hour	一時間 [ichi jikan]

in the morning	朝に [asa ni]	
early in the morning	早朝 [sōchō]	
this morning	今朝 [kesa]	
tomorrow morning	明日の朝 [ashita no asa]	

at noon	ランチのときに [ranchi no toki ni]	
in the afternoon	午後に [gogo ni]	
in the evening	夕方 [yūgata]	
tonight	今夜 [konya]	

at night	夜 [yoru]	
yesterday	昨日 [kinō]	
today	今日 [kyō]	
tomorrow	明日 [ashita]	
the day after tomorrow	あさって [asatte]	

What day is it today?	今日は何曜日ですか？ [kyō wa nan yōbi desu ka ?]	
It's …	…です [… desu]	
Monday	月曜日 [getsuyōbi]	
Tuesday	火曜日 [kayōbi]	
Wednesday	水曜日 [suiyōbi]	

Thursday	木曜日 [mokuyōbi]	
Friday	金曜日 [kinyōbi]	
Saturday	土曜日 [doyōbi]	
Sunday	日曜日 [nichiyōbi]	

Greetings. Introductions

Hello.
こんにちは。
[konnichiwa]

Pleased to meet you.
お会いできて嬉しいです。
[o aideki te ureshī desu]

Me too.
こちらこそ。
[kochira koso]

I'd like you to meet ...
…さんに会わせていただきたいのですが
[… san ni awasete itadaki tai no desu ga]

Nice to meet you.
初めまして。
[hajime mashite]

How are you?
お元気ですか？
[o genki desu ka ?]

My name is ...
私の名前は…です
[watashi no namae wa … desu]

His name is ...
彼の名前は…です
[kare no namae wa … desu]

Her name is ...
彼女の名前は…です
[kanojo no namae wa … desu]

What's your name?
お名前は何ですか？
[o namae wa nan desu ka ?]

What's his name?
彼の名前は何ですか？
[kare no namae wa nan desu ka ?]

What's her name?
彼女の名前は何ですか？
[kanojo no namae wa nan desu ka ?]

What's your last name?
苗字は何ですか？
[myōji wa nan desu ka ?]

You can call me ...
…と呼んで下さい
[… to yon de kudasai]

Where are you from?
ご出身はどちらですか？
[go shusshin wa dochira desu ka ?]

I'm from ...
…の出身です
[… no shusshin desu]

What do you do for a living?
お仕事は何をされていますか？
[o shigoto wa nani wo sare te i masu ka ?]

Who is this?
誰ですか？
[dare desu ka ?]

Who is he?
彼は誰ですか？
[kare wa dare desu ka ?]

Who is she?
彼女は誰ですか？
[kanojo wa dare desu ka ?]

Who are they?
彼らは誰ですか？
[karera wa dare desu ka ?]

This is ...
こちらは…
[kochira wa ...]

my friend (masc.)
私の友達です
[watashi no tomodachi desu]

my friend (fem.)
私の友達です
[watashi no tomodachi desu]

my husband
私の主人です
[watashi no shujin desu]

my wife
私の妻です
[watashi no tsuma desu]

my father
私の父です
[watashi no chichi desu]

my mother
私の母です
[watashi no haha desu]

my brother
私の兄です
[watashi no ani desu]

my sister
私の妹です
[watashi no imōto desu]

my son
私の息子です
[watashi no musuko desu]

my daughter
私の娘です
[watashi no musume desu]

This is our son.
私たちの息子です。
[watashi tachi no musuko desu]

This is our daughter.
私たちの娘です。
[watashi tachi no musume desu]

These are my children.
私の子供です。
[watashi no kodomo desu]

These are our children.
私たちの子供です。
[watashi tachi no kodomo desu]

Farewells

Good bye!
さようなら！
[sayōnara !]

Bye! (inform.)
じゃあね！
[jā ne !]

See you tomorrow.
また明日。
[mata ashita]

See you soon.
またね。
[mata ne]

See you at seven.
7時に会おう。
[shichi ji ni ao u]

Have fun!
楽しんでね！
[tanoshin de ne !]

Talk to you later.
じゃあ後で。
[jā atode]

Have a nice weekend.
良い週末を。
[yoi shūmatsu wo]

Good night.
お休みなさい。
[o yasuminasai]

It's time for me to go.
もう時間です。
[mō jikan desu]

I have to go.
もう行かなければなりません。
[mō ika nakere ba nari masen]

I will be right back.
すぐ戻ります。
[sugu modori masu]

It's late.
もう遅いです。
[mō osoi desu]

I have to get up early.
早く起きなければいけません。
[hayaku oki nakere ba ike masen]

I'm leaving tomorrow.
明日出発します。
[ashita shuppatsu shi masu]

We're leaving tomorrow.
私たちは明日出発します。
[watashi tachi wa ashita shuppatsu
shi masu]

Have a nice trip!
旅行を楽しんで下さい！
[ryokō wo tanoshin de kudasai !]

It was nice meeting you.
お会いできて嬉しかったです。
[o shiriai ni nare te uresikatta desu]

It was nice talking to you.
お話できて良かったです。
[ohanashi deki te yokatta desu]

Thanks for everything.　　　　　色々とありがとうございました。
　　　　　　　　　　　　　　　[iroiro to arigatō gozai mashi ta]

I had a very good time.　　　　　とても楽しかったです。
　　　　　　　　　　　　　　　[totemo tanoshikatta desu]

We had a very good time.　　　　とても楽しかったです。
　　　　　　　　　　　　　　　[totemo tanoshikatta desu]

It was really great.　　　　　　とても楽しかった。
　　　　　　　　　　　　　　　[totemo tanoshikatta]

I'm going to miss you.　　　　　寂しくなります。
　　　　　　　　　　　　　　　[sabishiku nari masu]

We're going to miss you.　　　　寂しくなります。
　　　　　　　　　　　　　　　[sabishiku nari masu]

Good luck!　　　　　　　　　幸運を祈るよ！
　　　　　　　　　　　　　　　[kōun wo inoru yo !]

Say hi to …　　　　　　　　　…に宜しくお伝え下さい。
　　　　　　　　　　　　　　　[… ni yoroshiku otsutae kudasai]

Foreign language

I don't understand.	分かりません。 [wakari masen]
Write it down, please.	それを書いて頂けますか？ [sore wo kai te itadake masu ka ?]
Do you speak …?	…語で話せますか？ [… go de hanase masu ka ?]

I speak a little bit of …	…を少し話せます […wo sukoshi hanase masu]
English	英語 [eigo]
Turkish	トルコ語 [toruko go]
Arabic	アラビア語 [arabia go]
French	フランス語 [furansu go]

German	ドイツ語 [doitsu go]
Italian	イタリア語 [itaria go]
Spanish	スペイン語 [supein go]
Portuguese	ポルトガル語 [porutogaru go]
Chinese	中国語 [chūgoku go]
Japanese	日本語 [nihon go]

Can you repeat that, please.	もう一度言っていただけますか。 [mōichido itte itadake masuka]
I understand.	分かりました。 [wakari mashi ta]
I don't understand.	分かりません。 [wakari masen]
Please speak more slowly.	もう少しゆっくり話して下さい。 [mōsukoshi yukkuri hanashi te kudasai]

Is that correct? (Am I saying it right?)	これで合っていますか？ [kore de atte i masu ka ?]
What is this? (What does this mean?)	これは何ですか？ [kore wa nan desu ka ?]

Apologies

Excuse me, please. すみませんがお願いします。
[sumimasen ga onegai shi masu]

I'm sorry. ごめんなさい。
[gomennasai]

I'm really sorry. 本当にごめんなさい。
[hontōni gomennasai]

Sorry, it's my fault. ごめんなさい、私のせいです。
[gomennasai, watashi no sei desu]

My mistake. 私の間違いでした。
[watashi no machigai deshi ta]

May I ...? …してもいいですか？
[… shi te mo ī desu ka ?]

Do you mind if I ...? …してもよろしいですか？
[… shi te mo yoroshī desu ka ?]

It's OK. 構いません。
[kamai masen]

It's all right. 大丈夫です。
[daijōbu desu]

Don't worry about it. それについては心配しないで下さい。
[sore ni tuitewa shinpai shi nai
de kudasai]

Agreement

Yes.
はい。
[hai]

Yes, sure.
はい、もちろん。
[hai, mochiron]

OK (Good!)
わかりました。
[wakari mashi ta]

Very well.
いいですよ。
[ī desuyo]

Certainly!
もちろん！
[mochiron !]

I agree.
賛成です。
[sansei desu]

That's correct.
それは正しい。
[sore wa tadashī]

That's right.
それは正しい。
[sore wa tadashī]

You're right.
あなたは合っています。
[anata wa atte imasu]

I don't mind.
気にしていません。
[kinisite imasen]

Absolutely right.
完全に正しいです。
[kanzen ni tadashī desu]

It's possible.
それは可能です。
[sore wa kanō desu]

That's a good idea.
それはいい考えです。
[sore wa ī kangae desu]

I can't say no.
断ることができません。
[kotowaru koto ga deki masen]

I'd be happy to.
喜んで。
[yorokon de]

With pleasure.
喜んで。
[yorokon de]

Refusal. Expressing doubt

No.	いいえ。 [īe]
Certainly not.	もちろん、違います。 [mochiron, chigai masu]
I don't agree.	賛成できません。 [sansei deki masen]
I don't think so.	そうは思いません。 [sō wa omoi masen]
It's not true.	それは事実ではありません。 [sore wa jijitsu de wa ari masen]

You are wrong.	あなたは間違っています。 [anata wa machigatte i masu]
I think you are wrong.	あなたは間違っていると思います。 [anata wa machigatte iru to omoi masu]
I'm not sure.	わかりません。 [wakari masen]
It's impossible.	それは不可能です。 [sore wa fukanō desu]
Nothing of the kind (sort)!	まさか！ [masaka !]

The exact opposite.	全く反対です。 [mattaku hantai desu]
I'm against it.	反対です。 [hantai desu]
I don't care.	構いません。 [kamai masen]
I have no idea.	全く分かりません。 [mattaku wakari masen]
I doubt that.	それはどうでしょう。 [sore wa dō desyō]

Sorry, I can't.	申し訳ありませんが、できません。 [mōshiwake arimasenga, deki masen]
Sorry, I don't want to.	申し訳ありませんが、遠慮させて いただきたいのです。 [mōshiwake arimasenga,ennryosasete itadakitai no desu]
Thank you, but I don't need this.	ありがとうございます。でもそれは 必要ではありません。 [arigatō gozai masu. demo sore wa hitsuyō de wa ari masen]

It's late.

もう遅いです。
[mō osoi desu]

I have to get up early.

早く起きなければいけません。
[hayaku oki nakere ba ike masen]

I don't feel well.

気分が悪いのです。
[kibun ga warui nodesu]

Expressing gratitude

Thank you.	ありがとうございます。 [arigatō gozai masu]
Thank you very much.	どうもありがとうございます。 [dōmo arigatō gozai masu]
I really appreciate it.	本当に感謝しています。 [hontōni kansha shi te i masu]
I'm really grateful to you.	あなたに本当に感謝しています。 [anata ni hontōni kansha shi te i masu]
We are really grateful to you.	私たちはあなたに本当に 感謝しています。 [watashi tachi wa anata ni hontōni kansha shi te i masu]

Thank you for your time.	お時間を頂きましてありがとう ございました。 [o jikan wo itadaki mashi te arigatō gozai mashi ta]
Thanks for everything.	何もかもありがとうございました。 [nanimokamo arigatō gozai mashi ta]
Thank you for ...	…をありがとうございます [... wo arigatō gozai masu]
your help	助けて頂いて [tasuke te itadai te]
a nice time	すばらしい時間 [subarashī jikan]

a wonderful meal	素敵なお料理 [suteki na o ryōri]
a pleasant evening	楽しい夜 [tanoshī yoru]
a wonderful day	素晴らしい 1日 [subarashī ichinichi]
an amazing journey	楽しい旅 [tanoshī tabi]

Don't mention it.	どういたしまして。 [dōitashimashite]
You are welcome.	どういたしまして。 [dōitashimashite]
Any time.	いつでもどうぞ。 [itsu demo dōzo]
My pleasure.	どういたしまして。 [dōitashimashite]

Forget it. It's alright.

忘れて下さい。
[wasure te kudasai]

Don't worry about it.

心配しないで下さい。
[shinpai shi nai de kudasai]

Congratulations. Best wishes

Congratulations!

おめでとうございます！
[omedetō gozai masu !]

Happy birthday!

お誕生日おめでとうございます！
[o tanjō bi omedetō gozai masu !]

Merry Christmas!

メリークリスマス！
[merīkurisumasu !]

Happy New Year!

新年明けましておめでとう
ございます！
[shinnen ake mashi te omedetō
gozai masu !]

Happy Easter!

イースターおめでとうございます！
[īsutā omedetō gozai masu !]

Happy Hanukkah!

ハヌカおめでとうございます！
[hanuka omedetō gozai masu !]

I'd like to propose a toast.

乾杯をあげたいです。
[kanpai wo age tai desu]

Cheers!

乾杯！
[kanpai !]

Let's drink to ...!

…のために乾杯しましょう！
[... no tame ni kanpai shi masho u !]

To our success!

我々の成功のために！
[wareware no seikō no tame ni !]

To your success!

あなたの成功のために！
[anata no seikō no tame ni !]

Good luck!

幸運を祈るよ！
[kōun wo inoru yo !]

Have a nice day!

良い一日をお過ごし下さい！
[yoi ichi nichi wo osugoshi kudasai !]

Have a good holiday!

良い休日をお過ごし下さい！
[yoi kyūjitsu wo osugoshi kudasai !]

Have a safe journey!

道中ご無事で！
[dōtyū gobujide!]

I hope you get better soon!

早く良くなるといいですね！
[hayaku yoku naru to ī desu ne !]

Socializing

Why are you sad?	なぜ悲しいのですか？ [naze kanashī no desu ka ?]
Smile! Cheer up!	笑って！　元気を出してください！ [waratte ! genki wo dashite kudasai !]
Are you free tonight?	今夜あいていますか？ [konya ai te i masu ka ?]
May I offer you a drink?	何か飲みますか？ [nani ka nomi masu ka ?]
Would you like to dance?	踊りませんか？ [odori masen ka ?]
Let's go to the movies.	映画に行きましょう。 [eiga ni iki masho u]
May I invite you to ...?	…へ誘ってもいいですか？ [… e sasotte mo ī desu ka ?]
a restaurant	レストラン [resutoran]
the movies	映画 [eiga]
the theater	劇場 [gekijō]
go for a walk	散歩 [sanpo]
At what time?	何時に？ [nan ji ni ?]
tonight	今晩 [konban]
at six	6時 [roku ji]
at seven	7時 [shichi ji]
at eight	8時 [hachi ji]
at nine	9時 [kyū ji]
Do you like it here?	ここが好きですか？ [koko ga suki desu ka ?]
Are you here with someone?	ここで誰かと一緒ですか？ [koko de dare ka to issyodesu ka ?]
I'm with my friend.	友達と一緒です。 [tomodachi to issho desu]

I'm with my friends.　友人たちと一緒です。
[yūjin tachi to issho desu]

No, I'm alone.　いいえ、一人です。
[īe, hitori desu]

Do you have a boyfriend?　彼氏いるの？
[kareshi iru no ?]

I have a boyfriend.　私は彼氏がいます。
[watashi wa kareshi ga i masu]

Do you have a girlfriend?　彼女いるの？
[kanojo iru no ?]

I have a girlfriend.　私は彼女がいます。
[watashi wa kanojo ga i masu]

Can I see you again?　また会えるかな？
[mata aeru ka na ?]

Can I call you?　電話してもいい？
[denwa shi te mo ī ?]

Call me. (Give me a call.)　電話してね。
[denwa shi te ne]

What's your number?　電話番号は？
[denwa bangō wa ?]

I miss you.　寂しくなるよ。
[sabishiku naru yo]

You have a beautiful name.　綺麗なお名前ですね。
[kirei na o namae desu ne]

I love you.　愛しているよ。
[aishi te iru yo]

Will you marry me?　結婚しようか
[kekkon shiyo u ka]

You're kidding!　冗談でしょう！
[jōdan dessyō!]

I'm just kidding.　冗談だよ。
[jōdan da yo]

Are you serious?　本気ですか？
[honki desuka ?]

I'm serious.　本気です。
[honki desu]

Really?!　本当ですか？！
[hontō desu ka ?!]

It's unbelievable!　信じられません！
[shinjirare masen !]

I don't believe you.　あなたは信じられません。
[anata wa shinzirare masen]

I can't.　私にはできません。
[watashi ni wa deki masen]

I don't know.　わかりません。
[wakari masen]

I don't understand you.　おっしゃることが分かりません。
[ossharu koto ga wakari masen]

Please go away. 出ていって下さい。
[de te itte kudasai]

Leave me alone! ほっといて下さい！
[hottoi te kudasai !]

I can't stand him. 彼には耐えられない。
[kare ni wa taerare nai]

You are disgusting! いやな人ですね！
[iyana hito desu ne !]

I'll call the police! 警察を呼びますよ！
[keisatsu wo yobi masuyo !]

Sharing impressions. Emotions

I like it.	これが好きです。 [kore ga suki desu]
Very nice.	とても素晴らしい。 [totemo subarashī]
That's great!	それはすばらしいです！ [sore wa subarashī desu !]
It's not bad.	それは悪くはないです。 [sore wa waruku wa nai desu]
I don't like it.	それが好きではありません。 [sore ga suki de wa ari masen]
It's not good.	それはよくないです。 [sore wa yoku nai desu]
It's bad.	それはひどいです。 [sore wa hidoi desu]
It's very bad.	それはとてもひどいです。 [sore wa totemo hidoi desu]
It's disgusting.	それは最悪です。 [sore wa saiaku desu]
I'm happy.	幸せです。 [shiawase desu]
I'm content.	満足しています。 [manzoku shi te i masu]
I'm in love.	好きな人がいます。 [suki na hito ga i masu]
I'm calm.	冷静です。 [reisei desu]
I'm bored.	退屈です。 [taikutsu desu]
I'm tired.	疲れています。 [tsukare te i masu]
I'm sad.	悲しいです。 [kanashī desu]
I'm frightened.	怖いです。 [kowai desu]
I'm angry.	腹が立ちます。 [haraga tachi masu]
I'm worried.	心配しています。 [shinpai shi te i masu]
I'm nervous.	緊張しています。 [kinchō shi te i masu]

I'm jealous. (envious)

嫉妬しています。
[shitto shi te i masu]

I'm surprised.

驚いています。
[odoroi te i masu]

I'm perplexed.

恥ずかしいです。
[hazukashī desu]

Problems. Accidents

I've got a problem.　　　　　　　困っています。
　　　　　　　　　　　　　　　　[komatte imasu]

We've got a problem.　　　　　　困っています。
　　　　　　　　　　　　　　　　[komatte imasu]

I'm lost.　　　　　　　　　　　　道に迷いました。
　　　　　　　　　　　　　　　　[michi ni mayoi mashi ta]

I missed the last bus (train).　　最終バス（電車）を逃しました。
　　　　　　　　　　　　　　　　[saishūbasu (densha) wo nogashi
　　　　　　　　　　　　　　　　mashi ta]

I don't have any money left.　　もうお金がありません。
　　　　　　　　　　　　　　　　[mō okane ga ari masen]

I've lost my ...　　　　　　　　…を失くしました
　　　　　　　　　　　　　　　　[... wo nakushi mashi ta]

Someone stole my ...　　　　　…を盗まれました
　　　　　　　　　　　　　　　　[... wo nusumare mashi ta]

passport　　　　　　　　　　　パスポート
　　　　　　　　　　　　　　　　[pasupōto]

wallet　　　　　　　　　　　　財布
　　　　　　　　　　　　　　　　[saifu]

papers　　　　　　　　　　　　書類
　　　　　　　　　　　　　　　　[shorui]

ticket　　　　　　　　　　　　切符
　　　　　　　　　　　　　　　　[kippu]

money　　　　　　　　　　　　お金
　　　　　　　　　　　　　　　　[okane]

handbag　　　　　　　　　　　ハンドバック
　　　　　　　　　　　　　　　　[handobakku]

camera　　　　　　　　　　　カメラ
　　　　　　　　　　　　　　　　[kamera]

laptop　　　　　　　　　　　ノートパソコン
　　　　　　　　　　　　　　　　[nōto pasokon]

tablet computer　　　　　　　タブレット型コンピューター
　　　　　　　　　　　　　　　　[taburetto gata konpyūtā]

mobile phone　　　　　　　　携帯電話
　　　　　　　　　　　　　　　　[keitai denwa]

Help me!　　　　　　　　　　助けて下さい！
　　　　　　　　　　　　　　　　[tasuke te kudasai !]

What's happened?　　　　　どうしましたか？
　　　　　　　　　　　　　　　　[dō shi mashi ta ka ?]

fire	火災 [kasai]
shooting	発砲 [happō]
murder	殺人 [satsujin]
explosion	爆発 [bakuhatsu]
fight	けんか [kenka]

Call the police!	警察を呼んで下さい！ [keisatsu wo yon de kudasai !]
Please hurry up!	急いで下さい！ [isoi de kudasai !]
I'm looking for the police station.	警察署を探しています。 [keisatsu sho wo sagashi te imasu]
I need to make a call.	電話をしなければなりません。 [denwa wo shi nakere ba nari masen]
May I use your phone?	お電話をお借りしても良いですか？ [o denwa wo o karishi te mo ī desu ka ?]

I've been ...	…されました [… sare mashi ta]
mugged	強盗 [gōtō]
robbed	盗まれる [nusumareru]
raped	レイプ [reipu]
attacked (beaten up)	暴行される [bōkō sareru]

Are you all right?	大丈夫ですか？ [daijōbu desu ka ?]
Did you see who it was?	誰が犯人か見ましたか？ [dare ga hanninn ka mi mashi ta ka ?]
Would you be able to recognize the person?	その人がどんな人か分かりますか？ [sono hito ga donna hito ka wakari masu ka?]
Are you sure?	本当に大丈夫ですか？ [hontōni daijōbu desu ka ?]

Please calm down.	落ち着いて下さい。 [ochitsui te kudasai]
Take it easy!	気楽に！ [kiraku ni !]
Don't worry!	心配しないで！ [shinpai shi nai de !]
Everything will be fine.	大丈夫ですから。 [daijōbu desu kara]

Everything's all right.

大丈夫ですから。
[daijōbu desu kara]

Come here, please.

こちらに来て下さい。
[kochira ni ki te kudasai]

I have some questions for you.

いくつかお伺いしたいことがあります。
[ikutuka o ukagai shi tai koto ga ari masu]

Wait a moment, please.

少しお待ち下さい。
[sukoshi omachi kudasai]

Do you have any I.D.?

身分証明書はお持ちですか？
[mibun shōmei sho wa o mochi desu ka ?]

Thanks. You can leave now.

ありがとうございます。もう
行っていいですよ。
[arigatō gozai masu. mō
itte ī desuyo]

Hands behind your head!

両手を頭の後ろで組みなさい！
[ryōute wo atama
no ushiro de kuminasai !]

You're under arrest!

逮捕します
[taiho shi masu]

Health problems

Please help me.	助けて下さい。 [tasuke te kudasai]
I don't feel well.	気分が悪いのです。 [kibun ga warui nodesu]
My husband doesn't feel well.	主人の具合が悪いのです。 [shujin no guai ga warui no desu]
My son ...	息子の… [musuko no ...]
My father ...	父の… [chichi no ...]
My wife doesn't feel well.	妻の具合が悪いのです。 [tsuma no guai ga warui no desu]
My daughter ...	娘の… [musume no ...]
My mother ...	母の… [haha no ...]
I've got a ...	…がします [... ga shi masu]
headache	頭痛 [zutsū]
sore throat	喉が痛い [nodo ga itai]
stomach ache	腹痛 [fukutsū]
toothache	歯痛 [shitsū]
I feel dizzy.	めまいがします。 [memai ga shi masu]
He has a fever.	彼は熱があります。 [kare wa netsu ga ari masu]
She has a fever.	彼女は熱があります。 [kanojo wa netsu ga ari masu]
I can't breathe.	息ができません。 [iki ga deki masen]
I'm short of breath.	息切れがします。 [ikigire ga shi masu]
I am asthmatic.	喘息です。 [zensoku desu]
I am diabetic.	糖尿病です。 [tōnyō byō desu]

I can't sleep. 不眠症です。
[huminsyō desu]

food poisoning 食中毒
[shokuchūdoku]

It hurts here. ここが痛いです。
[koko ga itai desu]

Help me! 助けて下さい！
[tasuke te kudasai !]

I am here! ここにいます！
[koko ni i masu !]

We are here! 私たちはここにいます！
[watashi tachi wa koko ni i masu !]

Get me out of here! ここから出して下さい！
[koko kara dashi te kudasai !]

I need a doctor. 医者に診せる必要があります。
[isha ni miseru hituyō ga arimasu]

I can't move. 動けません！
[ugoke masen !]

I can't move my legs. 足が動きません。
[ashi ga ugoki masen]

I have a wound. 傷があります。
[kizu ga ari masu]

Is it serious? それは重傷ですか？
[sore wa jūsyō desu ka ?]

My documents are in my pocket. 私に関する書類はポケッ
トに入っています。
[watashi nikansuru shorui wa poketto
ni haitte i masu]

Calm down! 落ち着いて下さい！
[ochitsui te kudasai !]

May I use your phone? お電話をお借りしても良いですか？
[o denwa wo o karishi te mo ī desu ka ?]

Call an ambulance! 救急車を呼んで下さい！
[kyūkyū sha wo yon de kudasai !]

It's urgent! 緊急です！
[kinkyū desu !]

It's an emergency! 緊急です！
[kinkyū desu !]

Please hurry up! 急いで下さい！
[isoi de kudasai !]

Would you please call a doctor? 医者を呼んでいただけますか？
[isha wo yon de itadake masu ka ?]

Where is the hospital? 病院はどこですか？
[byōin wa doko desu ka ?]

How are you feeling? ご気分はいかがですか？
[gokibun wa ikaga desu ka ?]

Are you all right? 大丈夫ですか？
[daijōbu desu ka ?]

What's happened?

どうしましたか？
[dō shi mashi ta ka ?]

I feel better now.

もう気分が良くなりました。
[mō kibun ga yoku narimashita]

It's OK.

大丈夫です。
[daijōbu desu]

It's all right.

大丈夫です。
[daijōbu desu]

At the pharmacy

pharmacy (drugstore)	薬局 [yakkyoku]
24-hour pharmacy	２４時間営業の薬局 [nijyū yo jikan eigyō no yakkyoku]
Where is the closest pharmacy?	一番近くの薬局はどこですか？ [ichiban chikaku no yakkyoku wa doko desu ka?]
Is it open now?	今開いていますか？ [ima ai te i masu ka ?]
At what time does it open?	何時に開きますか？ [nan ji ni aki masu ka ?]
At what time does it close?	何時に閉まりますか？ [nan ji ni shimari masu ka ?]
Is it far?	遠いですか？ [tōi desu ka ?]
Can I get there on foot?	そこまで歩いて行けますか？ [soko made arui te ike masu ka ?]
Can you show me on the map?	地図で教えて頂けますか？ [chizu de oshie te itadake masu ka ?]
Please give me something for ...	何か…に効くものを下さい [nani ka ... ni kiku mono wo kudasai]
a headache	頭痛 [zutsū]
a cough	咳 [seki]
a cold	風邪 [kaze]
the flu	インフルエンザ [infuruenza]
a fever	発熱 [hatsunetsu]
a stomach ache	胃痛 [itsū]
nausea	吐き気 [hakike]
diarrhea	下痢 [geri]
constipation	便秘 [benpi]

pain in the back	腰痛 [yōtsū]
chest pain	胸痛 [kyōtsū]
side stitch	脇腹の痛み [wakibara no itami]
abdominal pain	腹痛 [fukutsū]

pill	薬 [kusuri]
ointment, cream	軟膏、クリーム [nankō, kurīmu]
syrup	シロップ [shiroppu]
spray	スプレー [supurē]
drops	目薬 [megusuri]

You need to go to the hospital.	病院に行かなくてはなりません。 [byōin ni ika naku te wa nari masen]
health insurance	健康保険 [kenkō hoken]
prescription	処方箋 [shohōsen]
insect repellant	虫除け [mushiyoke]
Band Aid	絆創膏 [bansōkō]

The bare minimum

Excuse me, ...	すみません、… [sumimasen, ...]
Hello.	こんにちは。 [konnichiwa]
Thank you.	ありがとうございます。 [arigatō gozai masu]
Good bye.	さようなら。 [sayōnara]
Yes.	はい。 [hai]
No.	いいえ。 [īe]
I don't know.	わかりません。 [wakari masen]
Where? | Where to? | When?	どこ？ | どこへ？ | いつ？ [doko ? | doko e ? | i tsu ?]
I need ...	…が必要です [… ga hitsuyō desu]
I want ...	したいです [shi tai desu]
Do you have ...?	…をお持ちですか？ [… wo o mochi desu ka ?]
Is there a ... here?	ここには…がありますか？ [koko ni wa … ga ari masu ka ?]
May I ...?	…してもいいですか？ [… shi te mo ī desu ka ?]
..., please (polite request)	お願いします。 [onegai shi masu]
I'm looking for ...	…を探しています [… wo sagashi te i masu]
restroom	トイレ [toire]
ATM	ＡＴＭ [ētīemu]
pharmacy (drugstore)	薬局 [yakkyoku]
hospital	病院 [byōin]
police station	警察 [keisatsu]
subway	地下鉄 [chikatetsu]

taxi	タクシー [takushī]
train station	駅 [eki]

My name is ...	私は…と申します [watashi wa ... to mōshi masu]
What's your name?	お名前は何ですか？ [o namae wa nan desu ka ?]
Could you please help me?	助けていただけますか？ [tasuke te itadake masu ka ?]
I've got a problem.	困ったことがあります。 [komatta koto ga arimasu]
I don't feel well.	気分が悪いのです。 [kibun ga warui nodesu]
Call an ambulance!	救急車を呼んで下さい！ [kyūkyū sha wo yon de kudasai !]
May I make a call?	電話をしてもいいですか？ [denwa wo shi te mo ī desu ka ?]

I'm sorry.	ごめんなさい。 [gomennasai]
You're welcome.	どういたしまして。 [dōitashimashite]

I, me	私 [watashi]
you (inform.)	君 [kimi]
he	彼 [kare]
she	彼女 [kanojo]
they (masc.)	彼ら [karera]
they (fem.)	彼女たち [kanojotachi]
we	私たち [watashi tachi]
you (pl)	君たち [kimi tachi]
you (sg, form.)	あなた [anata]

ENTRANCE	入り口 [iriguchi]
EXIT	出口 [deguchi]
OUT OF ORDER	故障中 [koshō chū]
CLOSED	休業中 [kyūgyō chū]

OPEN
営業中
[eigyō chū]

FOR WOMEN
女性用
[josei yō]

FOR MEN
男性用
[dansei yō]

TOPICAL VOCABULARY

This section contains more than 3,000 of the most important words.
The dictionary will provide invaluable assistance while traveling abroad, because frequently individual words are enough for you to be understood.
The dictionary includes a convenient transcription of each foreign word

T&P Books Publishing

VOCABULARY
CONTENTS

T&P Books Publishing

BASIC CONCEPTS

T&P Books Publishing

1. Pronouns

I, me	私	watashi
you	あなた	anata
he	彼	kare
she	彼女	kanojo
we	私たち	watashi tachi
you (to a group)	あなたがた	anata ga ta
they	彼らは	karera wa

2. Greetings. Salutations

Hello! (fam.)	やあ！	yā!
Hello! (form.)	こんにちは！	konnichiwa!
Good morning!	おはよう！	ohayō!
Good afternoon!	こんにちは！	konnichiwa!
Good evening!	こんばんは！	konbanwa!
to say hello	こんにちはと言う	konnichiwa to iu
Hi! (hello)	やあ！	yā!
greeting (n)	挨拶	aisatsu
to greet (vt)	挨拶する	aisatsu suru
How are you?	元気？	genki?
How are you? (form.)	お元気ですか？	wo genki desu ka?
How are you? (fam.)	元気？	genki?
What's new?	調子はどう？	chōshi ha dō?
Bye-Bye! Goodbye!	さようなら！	sayōnara!
Goodbye! (form.)	さようなら！	sayōnara!
Bye! (fam.)	バイバイ！	baibai!
See you soon!	じゃあね！	jā ne!
Farewell!	さらば！	saraba!
to say goodbye	別れを告げる	wakare wo tsugeru
So long!	またね！	mata ne!
Thank you!	ありがとう！	arigatō!
Thank you very much!	どうもありがとう！	dōmo arigatō!
You're welcome	どういたしまして	dōitashimashite
Don't mention it!	礼なんていいよ	rei nante ī yo
It was nothing	どういたしまして	dōitashimashite
Excuse me! (fam.)	失礼！	shitsurei!
Excuse me! (form.)	失礼致します！	shitsurei itashi masu!

to excuse (forgive)	許す	yurusu
to apologize (vi)	謝る	ayamaru
My apologies	おわび致します！	owabi itashi masu!
I'm sorry!	ごめんなさい！	gomennasai!
to forgive (vt)	許す	yurusu
It's okay!	大丈夫です！	daijōbu desu!
please (adv)	お願い	onegai
Don't forget!	忘れないで！	wasure nai de!
Certainly!	もちろん！	mochiron!
Of course not!	そんなことないよ！	sonna koto nai yo!
Okay! (I agree)	オーケー！	ōkē!
That's enough!	もう十分だ！	mō jūbun da!

3. Questions

Who?	誰？	dare ?
What?	何？	nani ?
Where? (at, in)	どこに？	doko ni ?
Where (to)?	どちらへ？	dochira he ?
From where?	どこから？	doko kara ?
When?	いつ？	itsu ?
Why? (What for?)	なんで？	nande ?
Why? (reason)	どうして？	dōshite ?
What for?	何のために？	nan no tame ni ?
How? (in what way)	どうやって？	dō yatte?
What? (What kind of ...?)	どんな ？	donna?
Which?	どちらの…？	dochira no … ?
To whom?	誰に？	dare ni ?
About whom?	誰のこと？	dare no koto ?
About what?	何のこと？	nannokoto ?
With whom?	誰と？	dare to ?
How many?	いくつ？	ikutsu ?
How much?	いくら？	ikura ?
Whose?	誰のもの？	Dare no mono ?

4. Prepositions

with (accompanied by)	…と、…と共に	… to, totomoni
without	…なしで	… nashi de
to (indicating direction)	…へ	… he
about (talking ~ ...)	…について	… ni tsuite
before (in time)	…の前に	… no mae ni
in front of ...	…の正面に	… no shōmen ni
under (beneath, below)	下に	shita ni

above (over)	上側に	uwagawa ni
on (atop)	上に	ue ni
from (off, out of)	…から	… kara
of (made from)	…製の	… sei no
in (e.g., ~ ten minutes)	…で	… de
over (across the top of)	…を越えて	… wo koe te

5. Function words. Adverbs. Part 1

Where? (at, in)	どこに？	doko ni ?
here (adv)	ここで	kokode
there (adv)	そこで	sokode
somewhere (to be)	どこかで	doko ka de
nowhere (not anywhere)	どこにも	doko ni mo
by (near, beside)	近くで	chikaku de
by the window	窓辺に	mado beni
Where (to)?	どちらへ？	dochira he ?
here (e.g., come ~!)	こちらへ	kochira he
there (e.g., to go ~)	そこへ	soko he
from here (adv)	ここから	koko kara
from there (adv)	そこから	soko kara
close (adv)	そばに	soba ni
far (adv)	遠くに	tōku ni
near (e.g., ~ Paris)	近く	chikaku
nearby (adv)	近くに	chikaku ni
not far (adv)	遠くない	tōku nai
left (adj)	左の	hidari no
on the left	左に	hidari ni
to the left	左へ	hidari he
right (adj)	右の	migi no
on the right	右に	migi ni
to the right	右へ	migi he
in front (adv)	前に	mae ni
front (as adj)	前の	mae no
ahead (the kids ran ~)	前方へ	zenpō he
behind (adv)	後ろに	ushiro ni
from behind	後ろから	ushiro kara
back (towards the rear)	後ろへ	ushiro he
middle	中央	chūō
in the middle	中央に	chūō ni

at the side	側面から	sokumen kara
everywhere (adv)	どこでも	doko demo
around (in all directions)	…の周りを	… no mawari wo

from inside	中から	naka kara
somewhere (to go)	どこかへ	dokoka he
straight (directly)	真っ直ぐに	massugu ni
back (e.g., come ~)	戻って	modotte

| from anywhere | どこからでも | doko kara demo |
| from somewhere | どこからか | doko kara ka |

firstly (adv)	第一に	dai ichi ni
secondly (adv)	第二に	dai ni ni
thirdly (adv)	第三に	dai san ni

suddenly (adv)	急に	kyū ni
at first (at the beginning)	初めは	hajime wa
for the first time	初めて	hajimete
long before …	…かなり前に	…kanari mae ni
anew (over again)	新たに	arata ni
for good (adv)	永遠に	eien ni

never (adv)	一度も	ichi do mo
again (adv)	再び	futatabi
now (adv)	今	ima
often (adv)	よく	yoku
then (adv)	あのとき	ano toki
urgently (quickly)	至急に	shikyū ni
usually (adv)	普通は	futsū wa

by the way, …	ところで、…	tokorode, …
possible (that is ~)	可能な	kanō na
probably (adv)	恐らく［おそらく］	osoraku
maybe (adv)	ことによると	kotoni yoru to
besides …	それに	soreni
that's why …	従って	shitagatte
in spite of …	…にもかかわらず	… ni mo kakawara zu
thanks to …	…のおかげで	… no okage de

what (pron.)	何	nani
that (conj.)	…ということ	… toyuu koto
something	何か	nani ka
anything (something)	何か	nani ka
nothing	何もない	nani mo nai

who (pron.)	誰	dare
someone	ある人	aru hito
somebody	誰か	dare ka

| nobody | 誰も…ない | dare mo … nai |
| nowhere (a voyage to ~) | どこへも | doko he mo |

nobody's	誰の…でもない	dare no … de mo nai
somebody's	誰かの	dare ka no
so (I'm ~ glad)	とても	totemo
also (as well)	また	mata
too (as well)	も	mo

6. Function words. Adverbs. Part 2

Why?	どうして？	dōshite ?
for some reason	なぜか［何故か］	naze ka
because ...	なぜなら	nazenara
for some purpose	何らかの理由で	nanrakano riyū de
and	と	to
or	または	matawa
but	でも	demo
for (e.g., ~ me)	…のために	… no tame ni
too (~ many people)	…すぎる	… sugiru
only (exclusively)	もっぱら	moppara
exactly (adv)	正確に	seikaku ni
about (more or less)	約	yaku
approximately (adv)	おおよそ	ōyoso
approximate (adj)	おおよその	ōyosono
almost (adv)	ほとんど	hotondo
the rest	残り	nokori
the other (second)	もう一方の	mōippōno
other (different)	他の	hokano
each (adj)	各	kaku
any (no matter which)	どれでも	dore demo
many (adv)	多くの	ōku no
much (adv)	多量の	taryō no
many people	多くの人々	ōku no hitobito
all (everyone)	あらゆる人	arayuru hito
in return for ...	…の返礼として	… no henrei toshite
in exchange (adv)	引き換えに	hikikae ni
by hand (made)	手で	te de
hardly (negative opinion)	ほとんど…ない	hotondo … nai
probably (adv)	恐らく［おそらく］	osoraku
on purpose (intentionally)	わざと	wazato
by accident (adv)	偶然に	gūzen ni
very (adv)	非常に	hijō ni
for example (adv)	例えば	tatoeba
between	間	kan

among	…の間で	… no made
so much (such a lot)	たくさん	takusan
especially (adv)	特に	tokuni

NUMBERS.
MISCELLANEOUS

T&P Books Publishing

7. Cardinal numbers. Part 1

0 zero	ゼロ	zero
1 one	一	ichi
2 two	二	ni
3 three	三	san
4 four	四	yon
5 five	五	go
6 six	六	roku
7 seven	七	nana
8 eight	八	hachi
9 nine	九	kyū
10 ten	十	jū
11 eleven	十一	jū ichi
12 twelve	十二	jū ni
13 thirteen	十三	jū san
14 fourteen	十四	jū yon
15 fifteen	十五	jū go
16 sixteen	十六	jū roku
17 seventeen	十七	jū shichi
18 eighteen	十八	jū hachi
19 nineteen	十九	jū kyū
20 twenty	二十	ni jū
21 twenty-one	二十一	ni jū ichi
22 twenty-two	二十二	ni jū ni
23 twenty-three	二十三	ni jū san
30 thirty	三十	san jū
31 thirty-one	三一	san jū ichi
32 thirty-two	三二	san jū ni
33 thirty-three	三三	san jū san
40 forty	四十	yon jū
41 forty-one	四一	yon jū ichi
42 forty-two	四二	yon jū ni
43 forty-three	四三	yon jū san
50 fifty	五十	go jū
51 fifty-one	五十一	go jū ichi
52 fifty-two	五十二	go jū ni
53 fifty-three	五十三	go jū san
60 sixty	六十	roku jū

61 sixty-one	六十一	roku jū ichi
62 sixty-two	六十二	roku jū ni
63 sixty-three	六十三	roku jū san

70 seventy	七十	nana jū
71 seventy-one	七十一	nana jū ichi
72 seventy-two	七十二	nana jū ni
73 seventy-three	七十三	nana jū san

80 eighty	八十	hachi jū
81 eighty-one	八十一	hachi jū ichi
82 eighty-two	八十二	hachi jū ni
83 eighty-three	八十三	hachi jū san

90 ninety	九十	kyū jū
91 ninety-one	九十一	kyū jū ichi
92 ninety-two	九十二	kyū jū ni
93 ninety-three	九十三	kyū jū san

8. Cardinal numbers. Part 2

100 one hundred	百	hyaku
200 two hundred	二百	ni hyaku
300 three hundred	三百	san byaku
400 four hundred	四百	yon hyaku
500 five hundred	五百	go hyaku

600 six hundred	六百	roppyaku
700 seven hundred	七百	nana hyaku
800 eight hundred	八百	happyaku
900 nine hundred	九百	kyū hyaku

1000 one thousand	千	sen
2000 two thousand	二千	nisen
3000 three thousand	三千	sanzen
10000 ten thousand	一万	ichiman
one hundred thousand	１０万	jyūman
million	百万	hyakuman
billion	十億	jūoku

9. Ordinal numbers

first (adj)	第一の	dai ichi no
second (adj)	第二の	dai ni no
third (adj)	第三の	dai san no
fourth (adj)	第四の	dai yon no
fifth (adj)	第五の	dai go no
sixth (adj)	第六の	dai roku no

seventh (adj)	第七の	dai nana no
eighth (adj)	第八の	dai hachi no
ninth (adj)	第九の	dai kyū no
tenth (adj)	第十の	dai jū no

COLOURS. UNITS OF MEASUREMENT

T&P Books Publishing

10. Colors

color	色	iro
shade (tint)	色合い	iroai
hue	色相	shikisō
rainbow	虹	niji

white (adj)	白い	shiroi
black (adj)	黒い	kuroi
gray (adj)	灰色の	haīro no

green (adj)	緑の	midori no
yellow (adj)	黄色い	kīroi
red (adj)	赤い	akai
blue (adj)	青い	aoi
light blue (adj)	水色の	mizu iro no
pink (adj)	ピンクの	pinku no
orange (adj)	オレンジの	orenji no
violet (adj)	紫色の	murasaki iro no
brown (adj)	茶色の	chairo no

golden (adj)	金色の	kiniro no
silvery (adj)	銀色の	giniro no
beige (adj)	ベージュの	bēju no
cream (adj)	クリームの	kurīmu no
turquoise (adj)	ターコイズブルーの	tākoizuburū no
cherry red (adj)	チェリーレッドの	cherī reddo no
lilac (adj)	ライラックの	rairakku no
crimson (adj)	クリムゾンの	kurimuzon no

light (adj)	薄い	usui
dark (adj)	濃い	koi
bright, vivid (adj)	鮮やかな	azayaka na

colored (pencils)	色の	iro no
color (e.g., ~ film)	カラー…	karā...
black-and-white (adj)	白黒の	shirokuro no
plain (one-colored)	単色の	tanshoku no
multicolored (adj)	色とりどりの	irotoridori no

11. Units of measurement

weight	重さ	omo sa
length	長さ	naga sa

width	幅	haba
height	高さ	taka sa
depth	深さ	fuka sa
volume	体積	taiseki
area	面積	menseki

gram	グラム	guramu
milligram	ミリグラム	miriguramu
kilogram	キログラム	kiroguramu
ton	トン	ton
pound	ポンド	pondo
ounce	オンス	onsu

meter	メートル	mētoru
millimeter	ミリメートル	mirimētoru
centimeter	センチメートル	senchimētoru
kilometer	キロメートル	kiromētoru
mile	マイル	mairu

inch	インチ	inchi
foot	フィート	fīto
yard	ヤード	yādo

square meter	平方メートル	heihō mētoru
hectare	ヘクタール	hekutāru
liter	リットル	rittoru
degree	度	do
volt	ボルト	boruto
ampere	アンペア	anpea
horsepower	馬力	bariki

quantity	数量	sūryō
a little bit of ...	少し	sukoshi
half	半分	hanbun
dozen	ダース	dāsu
piece (item)	一個	ikko

| size | 大きさ | ōki sa |
| scale (map ~) | 縮尺 | shukushaku |

minimal (adj)	極小の	kyokushō no
the smallest (adj)	最小の	saishō no
medium (adj)	中位の	chūi no
maximal (adj)	極大の	kyokudai no
the largest (adj)	最大の	saidai no

12. Containers

| canning jar (glass ~) | ジャー、瓶 | jā, bin |
| can | 缶 | kan |

bucket	バケツ	baketsu
barrel	樽	taru
wash basin (e.g., plastic ~)	たらい ［盥］	tarai
tank (100 - 200L water ~)	タンク	tanku
hip flask	スキットル	sukittoru
jerrycan	ジェリカン	jerikan
tank (e.g., tank car)	積荷タンク	tsumini tanku
mug	マグカップ	magukappu
cup (of coffee, etc.)	カップ	kappu
saucer	ソーサー	sōsā
glass (tumbler)	ガラスのコップ	garasu no koppu
wine glass	ワイングラス	wain gurasu
stock pot (soup pot)	両手鍋	ryō tenabe
bottle (~ of wine)	ボトル	botoru
neck (of the bottle, etc.)	ネック	nekku
carafe	デキャンター	dekyanta
pitcher	水差し	mizusashi
vessel (container)	器	utsuwa
pot (crock, stoneware ~)	鉢	hachi
vase	花瓶	kabin
bottle (perfume ~)	瓶	bin
vial, small bottle	バイアル	bai aru
tube (of toothpaste)	チューブ	chūbu
sack (bag)	南京袋	nankinbukuro
bag (paper ~, plastic ~)	袋	fukuro
pack (of cigarettes, etc.)	箱	hako
box (e.g., shoebox)	箱	hako
crate	木箱	ki bako
basket	かご ［籠］	kago

MAIN VERBS

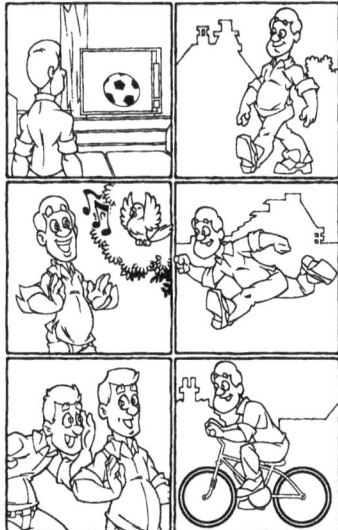

T&P Books Publishing

to advise (vt)	助言する	jogen suru
to agree (say yes)	同意する	dōi suru
to answer (vi, vt)	回答する	kaitō suru
to apologize (vi)	謝る	ayamaru
to arrive (vi)	到着する	tōchaku suru
to ask (~ oneself)	問う	tō
to ask (~ sb to do sth)	頼む	tanomu
to be (vi)	ある	aru
to be afraid	怖がる	kowagaru
to be hungry	腹をすかす	hara wo sukasu
to be interested in ...	…に興味がある	... ni kyōmi ga aru
to be needed	必要である	hitsuyō de aru
to be surprised	驚く	odoroku
to be thirsty	喉が渇く	nodo ga kawaku
to begin (vt)	始める	hajimeru
to belong to ...	所有物である	shoyū butsu de aru
to boast (vi)	自慢する	jiman suru
to break (split into pieces)	折る、壊す	oru, kowasu
to call (~ for help)	求める	motomeru
can (v aux)	できる	dekiru
to catch (vt)	捕らえる	toraeru
to change (vt)	変える	kaeru
to choose (select)	選択する	sentaku suru
to come down (the stairs)	下りる	oriru
to compare (vt)	比較する	hikaku suru
to complain (vi, vt)	不平を言う	fuhei wo iu
to confuse (mix up)	混同する	kondō suru
to continue (vt)	続ける	tsuzukeru
to control (vt)	管制する	kansei suru
to cook (dinner)	料理をする	ryōri wo suru
to cost (vt)	かかる	kakaru
to count (add up)	計算する	keisan suru
to count on ...	…を頼りにする	... wo tayori ni suru
to create (vt)	創造する	sōzō suru
to cry (weep)	泣く	naku

14. The most important verbs. Part 2

to deceive (vi, vt)	だます	damasu
to decorate (tree, street)	飾る	kazaru
to defend (a country, etc.)	防衛する	bōei suru
to demand (request firmly)	要求する	yōkyū suru
to dig (vt)	掘る	horu
to discuss (vt)	討議する	tōgi suru
to do (vt)	する	suru
to doubt (have doubts)	疑う	utagau
to drop (let fall)	落とす	otosu
to enter (room, house, etc.)	入る	hairu
to excuse (forgive)	許す	yurusu
to exist (vi)	存在する	sonzai suru
to expect (foresee)	見越す	mikosu
to explain (vt)	説明する	setsumei suru
to fall (vi)	落ちる	ochiru
to find (vt)	見つける	mitsukeru
to finish (vt)	終える	oeru
to fly (vi)	飛ぶ	tobu
to follow ... (come after)	…について行く	… ni tsuiteiku
to forget (vi, vt)	忘れる	wasureru
to forgive (vt)	許す	yurusu
to give (vt)	手渡す	tewatasu
to give a hint	暗示する	anji suru
to go (on foot)	行く	iku
to go for a swim	海水浴をする	kaisuiyoku wo suru
to go out (for dinner, etc.)	出る	deru
to guess (the answer)	言い当てる	īateru
to have (vt)	持つ	motsu
to have breakfast	朝食をとる	chōshoku wo toru
to have dinner	夕食をとる	yūshoku wo toru
to have lunch	昼食をとる	chūshoku wo toru
to hear (vt)	聞く	kiku
to help (vt)	手伝う	tetsudau
to hide (vt)	隠す	kakusu
to hope (vi, vt)	希望する	kibō suru
to hunt (vi, vt)	狩る	karu
to hurry (vi)	急ぐ	isogu

15.   The most important verbs. Part 3

to inform (vt)	知らせる	shiraseru
to insist (vi, vt)	主張する	shuchō suru
to insult (vt)	侮辱する	bujoku suru
to invite (vt)	招待する	shōtai suru
to joke (vi)	冗談を言う	jōdan wo iu
to keep (vt)	保つ	tamotsu
to keep silent	沈黙を守る	chinmoku wo mamoru
to kill (vt)	殺す	korosu
to know (sb)	知っている	shitte iru
to know (sth)	知る	shiru
to laugh (vi)	笑う	warau
to liberate (city, etc.)	解放する	kaihō suru
to like (I like ...)	好む	konomu
to look for ... (search)	探す	sagasu
to love (sb)	愛する	aisuru
to make a mistake	誤りをする	ayamari wo suru
to manage, to run	管理する	kanri suru
to mean (signify)	意味する	imi suru
to mention (talk about)	言及する	genkyū suru
to miss (school, etc.)	欠席する	kesseki suru
to notice (see)	見掛ける	mikakeru
to object (vi, vt)	反対する	hantai suru
to observe (see)	監視する	kanshi suru
to open (vt)	開ける	akeru
to order (meal, etc.)	注文する	chūmon suru
to order (mil.)	命令する	meirei suru
to own (possess)	所有する	shoyū suru
to participate (vi)	参加する	sanka suru
to pay (vi, vt)	払う	harau
to permit (vt)	許可する	kyoka suru
to plan (vt)	計画する	keikaku suru
to play (children)	遊ぶ	asobu
to pray (vi, vt)	祈る	inoru
to prefer (vt)	好む	konomu
to promise (vt)	約束する	yakusoku suru
to pronounce (vt)	発音する	hatsuon suru
to propose (vt)	提案する	teian suru
to punish (vt)	罰する	bassuru

16.   The most important verbs. Part 4

to read (vi, vt)	読む	yomu
to recommend (vt)	推薦する	suisen suru
to refuse (vi, vt)	拒絶する	kyozetsu suru

to regret (be sorry)	後悔する	kōkai suru
to rent (sth from sb)	借りる	kariru
to repeat (say again)	復唱する	fukushō suru
to reserve, to book	予約する	yoyaku suru
to run (vi)	走る	hashiru
to save (rescue)	救出する	kyūshutsu suru
to say (~ thank you)	言う	iu
to scold (vt)	叱る [しかる]	shikaru
to see (vt)	見る	miru
to sell (vt)	売る	uru
to send (vt)	送る	okuru
to shoot (vi)	撃つ	utsu
to shout (vi)	叫ぶ	sakebu
to show (vt)	見せる	miseru
to sign (document)	署名する	shomei suru
to sit down (vi)	座る	suwaru
to smile (vi)	ほほえむ [微笑む]	hohoemu
to speak (vi, vt)	話す	hanasu
to steal (money, etc.)	盗む	nusumu
to stop (for pause, etc.)	止まる	tomaru
to stop (please ~ calling me)	止める	tomeru
to study (vt)	勉強する	benkyō suru
to swim (vi)	泳ぐ	oyogu
to take (vt)	取る	toru
to think (vi, vt)	思う	omō
to threaten (vt)	威す	odosu
to touch (with hands)	触れる	fureru
to translate (vt)	翻訳する	honyaku suru
to trust (vt)	信用する	shinyō suru
to try (attempt)	試みる	kokoromiru
to turn (e.g., ~ left)	曲がる	magaru
to underestimate (vt)	甘く見る	amaku miru
to understand (vt)	理解する	rikai suru
to unite (vt)	合体させる	gattai saseru
to wait (vt)	待つ	matsu
to want (wish, desire)	欲する	hossuru
to warn (vt)	警告する	keikoku suru
to work (vi)	働く	hataraku
to write (vt)	書く	kaku
to write down	書き留める	kakitomeru

T&P BOOKS

TIME. CALENDAR

T&P Books Publishing

17. Weekdays

Monday	月曜日	getsuyōbi
Tuesday	火曜日	kayōbi
Wednesday	水曜日	suiyōbi
Thursday	木曜日	mokuyōbi
Friday	金曜日	kinyōbi
Saturday	土曜日	doyōbi
Sunday	日曜日	nichiyōbi
today (adv)	今日	kyō
tomorrow (adv)	明日	ashita
the day after tomorrow	明後日 ［あさって］	asatte
yesterday (adv)	昨日	kinō
the day before yesterday	一昨日 ［おととい］	ototoi
day	日	nichi
working day	営業日	eigyōbi
public holiday	公休	kōkyū
day off	休み	yasumi
weekend	週末	shūmatsu
all day long	一日中	ichi nichi chū
the next day (adv)	翌日	yokujitsu
two days ago	2日前に	futsu ka mae ni
the day before	その前日に	sono zenjitsu ni
daily (adj)	毎日の	mainichi no
every day (adv)	毎日	mainichi
week	週	shū
last week (adv)	先週	senshū
next week (adv)	来週	raishū
weekly (adj)	毎週の	maishū no
every week (adv)	毎週	maishū
twice a week	週に2回	shūni nikai
every Tuesday	毎週火曜日	maishū kayōbi

18. Hours. Day and night

morning	朝	asa
in the morning	朝に	asa ni
noon, midday	正午	shōgo
in the afternoon	午後に	gogo ni
evening	夕方	yūgata

in the evening	夕方に	yūgata ni
night	夜	yoru
at night	夜に	yoru ni
midnight	真夜中	mayonaka

second	秒	byō
minute	分	fun, pun
hour	時間	jikan
half an hour	３０分	san jū fun
a quarter-hour	１５分	jū go fun
fifteen minutes	１５分	jū go fun
24 hours	一昼夜	icchūya

sunrise	日の出	hinode
dawn	夜明け	yoake
early morning	早朝	sōchō
sunset	夕日	yūhi

early in the morning	早朝に	sōchō ni
this morning	今朝	kesa
tomorrow morning	明日の朝	ashita no asa

this afternoon	今日の午後	kyō no gogo
in the afternoon	午後	gogo
tomorrow afternoon	明日の午後	ashita no gogo

| tonight (this evening) | 今夜 | konya |
| tomorrow night | 明日の夜 | ashita no yoru |

at 3 o'clock sharp	３時ちょうどに	sanji chōdo ni
about 4 o'clock	４時頃	yoji goro
by 12 o'clock	１２時までに	jūniji made ni

in 20 minutes	２０分後	nijuppungo
in an hour	一時間後	ichi jikan go
on time (adv)	予定通りに	yotei dōri ni

a quarter of …	…時１５分	… ji jyūgo fun
within an hour	１時間で	ichi jikan de
every 15 minutes	１５分ごとに	jyūgo fun goto ni
round the clock	昼も夜も	hiru mo yoru mo

19. Months. Seasons

January	一月	ichigatsu
February	二月	nigatsu
March	三月	sangatsu
April	四月	shigatsu
May	五月	gogatsu
June	六月	rokugatsu

July	七月	shichigatsu
August	八月	hachigatsu
September	九月	kugatsu
October	十月	jūgatsu
November	十一月	jūichigatsu
December	十二月	jūnigatsu

spring	春	haru
in spring	春に	haru ni
spring (as adj)	春の	haru no

summer	夏	natsu
in summer	夏に	natsu ni
summer (as adj)	夏の	natsu no

fall	秋	aki
in fall	秋に	aki ni
fall (as adj)	秋の	aki no

winter	冬	fuyu
in winter	冬に	fuyu ni
winter (as adj)	冬の	fuyu no

month	月	tsuki
this month	今月	kongetsu
next month	来月	raigetsu
last month	先月	sengetsu

a month ago	一ヶ月前	ichi kagetsu mae
in a month (a month later)	一ヶ月後	ichi kagetsu go
in 2 months (2 months later)	二ヶ月後	ni kagetsu go
the whole month	丸一ヶ月	maru ichi kagetsu
all month long	一ヶ月間ずっと	ichi kagetsu kan zutto

monthly (~ magazine)	月刊の	gekkan no
monthly (adv)	毎月	maitsuki
every month	月1回	tsuki ichi kai
twice a month	月に2回	tsuki ni ni kai

year	年	nen
this year	今年	kotoshi
next year	来年	rainen
last year	去年	kyonen

a year ago	一年前	ichi nen mae
in a year	一年後	ichi nen go
in two years	二年後	ni nen go
the whole year	丸一年	maru ichi nen
all year long	通年	tsūnen
every year	毎年	maitoshi
annual (adj)	毎年の	maitoshi no

annually (adv)	年1回	toshi ichi kai
4 times a year	年に4回	toshi ni yon kai
date (e.g., today's ~)	日付	hizuke
date (e.g., ~ of birth)	年月日	nengappi
calendar	カレンダー	karendā
half a year	半年	hantoshi
six months	6ヶ月	roku kagetsu
season (summer, etc.)	季節	kisetsu
century	世紀	seiki

TRAVEL. HOTEL

T&P Books Publishing

20. Trip. Travel

tourism, travel	観光	kankō
tourist	観光客	kankō kyaku
trip, voyage	旅行	ryokō
adventure	冒険	bōken
trip, journey	旅	tabi
vacation	休暇	kyūka
to be on vacation	休暇中です	kyūka chū desu
rest	休み	yasumi
train	列車	ressha
by train	列車で	ressha de
airplane	航空機	kōkūki
by airplane	飛行機で	hikōki de
by car	車で	kuruma de
by ship	船で	fune de
luggage	荷物	nimotsu
suitcase	スーツケース	sūtsukēsu
luggage cart	荷物カート	nimotsu kāto
passport	パスポート	pasupōto
visa	ビザ	biza
ticket	乗車券	jōsha ken
air ticket	航空券	kōkū ken
guidebook	ガイドブック	gaido bukku
map (tourist ~)	地図	chizu
area (rural ~)	地域	chīki
place, site	場所	basho
exotica (n)	エキゾチック	ekizochikku
exotic (adj)	エキゾチックな	ekizochikku na
amazing (adj)	驚くべき	odoroku beki
group	団	dan
excursion, sightseeing tour	小旅行	shō ryokō
guide (person)	ツアーガイド	tuā gaido

21. Hotel

hotel	ホテル	hoteru
motel	モーテル	mō teru

three-star	三つ星	mitsu boshi
five-star	五つ星	itsutsu boshi
to stay (in hotel, etc.)	泊まる	tomaru

room	部屋、ルーム	heya, rūmu
single room	シングルルーム	shinguru rūmu
double room	ダブルルーム	daburu rūmu
to book a room	部屋を予約する	heya wo yoyaku suru

| half board | ハーフボード | hāfu bōdo |
| full board | フルボード | furu bōdo |

with bath	浴槽付きの	yokusō tsuki no
with shower	シャワー付きの	shawā tsuki no
satellite television	衛星テレビ	eisei terebi
air-conditioner	エアコン	eakon
towel	タオル	taoru
key	鍵	kagi

administrator	管理人	kanri jin
chambermaid	客室係	kyakushitsu gakari
porter, bellboy	ベルボーイ	beru bōi
doorman	ドアマン	doa man

restaurant	レストラン	resutoran
pub, bar	パブ、バー	pabu, bā
breakfast	朝食	chōshoku
dinner	夕食	yūshoku
buffet	ビュッフェ	byuffe

| lobby | ロビー | robī |
| elevator | エレベーター | erebētā |

| DO NOT DISTURB | 起こさないで下さい | okosa nai de kudasai |
| NO SMOKING | 禁煙 | kinen |

22. Sightseeing

monument	記念碑	kinen hi
fortress	要塞	yōsai
palace	宮殿	kyūden
castle	城	shiro
tower	塔	tō
mausoleum	マウソレウム	mausoreumu

architecture	建築	kenchiku
medieval (adj)	中世の	chūsei no
ancient (adj)	古代の	kodai no
national (adj)	国の	kuni no
well-known (adj)	有名な	yūmei na

tourist	観光客	kankō kyaku
guide (person)	ガイド	gaido
excursion, sightseeing tour	小旅行	shō ryokō
to show (vt)	案内する	annai suru
to tell (vt)	話をする	hanashi wo suru

to find (vt)	見つける	mitsukeru
to get lost (lose one's way)	道に迷う	michi ni mayō
map (e.g., subway ~)	地図	chizu
map (e.g., city ~)	地図	chizu

souvenir, gift	土産	miyage
gift shop	土産品店	miyage hin ten
to take pictures	写真に撮る	shashin ni toru
to have one's picture taken	写真を撮られる	shashin wo torareru

T&P BOOKS

TRANSPORTATION

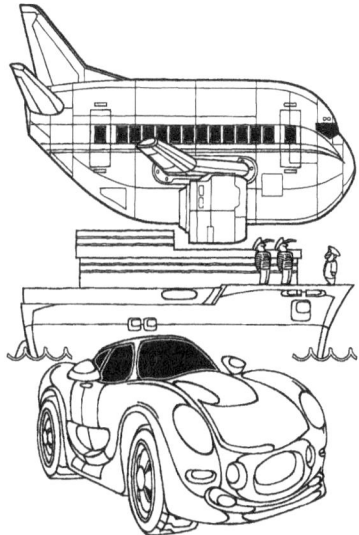

T&P Books Publishing

airport	空港	kūkō
airplane	航空機	kōkūki
airline	航空会社	kōkū gaisha
air traffic controller	航空管制官	kōkū kansei kan
departure	出発	shuppatsu
arrival	到着	tōchaku
to arrive (by plane)	到着する	tōchaku suru
departure time	出発時刻	shuppatsu jikoku
arrival time	到着時刻	tōchaku jikoku
to be delayed	遅れる	okureru
flight delay	フライトの遅延	furaito no chien
information board	フライト情報	furaito jōhō
information	案内	annai
to announce (vt)	アナウンスする	anaunsu suru
flight (e.g., next ~)	フライト	furaito
customs	税関	zeikan
customs officer	税関吏	zeikanri
customs declaration	税関申告	zeikan shinkoku
to fill out (vt)	記入する	kinyū suru
to fill out the declaration	申告書を記入する	shinkoku sho wo kinyū suru
passport control	入国審査	nyūkoku shinsa
luggage	荷物	nimotsu
hand luggage	持ち込み荷物	mochikomi nimotsu
Lost Luggage Desk	荷物紛失窓口	nimotsu funshitsu madoguchi
luggage cart	荷物カート	nimotsu kāto
landing	着陸	chakuriku
landing strip	滑走路	kassō ro
to land (vi)	着陸する	chakuriku suru
airstairs	タラップ	tarappu
check-in	チェックイン	chekkuin
check-in desk	チェックインカウンター	chekkuin kauntā
to check-in (vi)	チェックインする	chekkuin suru
boarding pass	搭乗券	tōjō ken

departure gate	出発ゲート	shuppatsu gēto
transit	乗り継ぎ	noritsugi
to wait (vt)	待つ	matsu
departure lounge	出発ロビー	shuppatsu robī
to see off	見送る	miokuru
to say goodbye	別れを告げる	wakare wo tsugeru

24. Airplane

airplane	航空機	kōkūki
air ticket	航空券	kōkū ken
airline	航空会社	kōkū gaisha
airport	空港	kūkō
supersonic (adj)	超音速の	chō onsoku no
captain	機長	kichō
crew	乗務員	jōmu in
pilot	パイロット	pairotto
flight attendant	客室乗務員	kyakushitsu jōmu in
navigator	航空士	kōkū shi
wings	翼	tsubasa
tail	尾部	o bu
cockpit	コックピット	kokkupitto
engine	エンジン	enjin
undercarriage (landing gear)	着陸装置	chakuriku sōchi
turbine	タービン	tābin
propeller	プロペラ	puropera
black box	ブラックボックス	burakku bokkusu
yoke (control column)	操縦ハンドル	sōjū handoru
fuel	燃料	nenryō
safety card	安全のしおり	anzen no shiori
oxygen mask	酸素マスク	sanso masuku
uniform	制服	seifuku
life vest	ライフジャケット	raifu jaketto
parachute	落下傘	rakkasan
takeoff	離陸	ririku
to take off (vi)	離陸する	ririku suru
runway	滑走路	kassō ro
visibility	視程	shitei
flight (act of flying)	飛行	hikō
altitude	高度	kōdo
air pocket	エアポケット	eapoketto
seat	席	seki
headphones	ヘッドホン	heddohon

folding tray (tray table)	折りたたみ式の テーブル	oritatami shiki no tēburu
airplane window	機窓	kisō
aisle	通路	tsūro

25. Train

train	列車	ressha
commuter train	通勤列車	tsūkin ressha
express train	高速鉄道	kōsoku tetsudō
diesel locomotive	ディーゼル機関車	dīzeru kikan sha
steam locomotive	蒸気機関車	jōki kikan sha
passenger car	客車	kyakusha
dining car	食堂車	shokudō sha
rails	レール	rēru
railroad	鉄道	tetsudō
railway tie	枕木	makuragi
platform (railway ~)	ホーム	hōmu
track (~ 1, 2, etc.)	線路	senro
semaphore	鉄道信号機	tetsudō shingō ki
station	駅	eki
engineer (train driver)	機関士	kikan shi
porter (of luggage)	ポーター	pōtā
car attendant	車掌	shashō
passenger	乗客	jōkyaku
conductor (ticket inspector)	検札係	kensatsu gakari
corridor (in train)	通路	tsūro
emergency brake	非常ブレーキ	hijō burēki
compartment	コンパートメント	konpātomento
berth	寝台	shindai
upper berth	上段寝台	jōdan shindai
lower berth	下段寝台	gedan shindai
bed linen, bedding	リネン	rinen
ticket	乗車券	jōsha ken
schedule	時刻表	jikoku hyō
information display	発車標	hassha shirube
to leave, to depart	発車する	hassha suru
departure (of train)	発車	hassha
to arrive (ab. train)	到着する	tōchaku suru
arrival	到着	tōchaku
to arrive by train	電車で来る	densha de kuru

| to get on the train | 電車に乗る | densha ni noru |
| to get off the train | 電車をおりる | densha wo oriru |

train wreck	鉄道事故	tetsudō jiko
to derail (vi)	脱線する	dassen suru
steam locomotive	蒸気機関車	jōki kikan sha
stoker, fireman	火夫	kafu
firebox	火室	kashitsu
coal	石炭	sekitan

26. Ship

| ship | 船舶 | senpaku |
| vessel | 大型船 | ōgata sen |

steamship	蒸気船	jōki sen
riverboat	川船	kawabune
cruise ship	遠洋定期船	enyō teiki sen
cruiser	クルーザー	kurūzā

yacht	ヨット	yotto
tugboat	曳船	eisen
barge	艀、バージ	hashike, bāji
ferry	フェリー	ferī

| sailing ship | 帆船 | hansen |
| brigantine | ブリガンティン | burigantin |

| ice breaker | 砕氷船 | saihyō sen |
| submarine | 潜水艦 | sensui kan |

boat (flat-bottomed ~)	ボート	bōto
dinghy	ディンギー	dingī
lifeboat	救命艇	kyūmei tei
motorboat	モーターボート	mōtābōto

captain	船長	senchō
seaman	船員	senin
sailor	水夫	suifu
crew	乗組員	norikumi in

boatswain	ボースン	bōsun
ship's boy	キャビンボーイ	kyabin bōi
cook	船のコック	fune no kokku
ship's doctor	船医	seni

deck	甲板	kanpan
mast	マスト	masuto
sail	帆	ho
hold	船倉	funagura

bow (prow)	船首	senshu
stern	船尾	senbi
oar	櫂	kai
screw propeller	プロペラ	puropera

cabin	船室	senshitsu
wardroom	士官室	shikan shitsu
engine room	機関室	kikan shitsu
bridge	船橋	funabashi
radio room	無線室	musen shitsu
wave (radio)	電波	denpa
logbook	航海日誌	kōkai nisshi

spyglass	単眼望遠鏡	tangan bōenkyō
bell	船鐘	funekane
flag	旗	hata

| rope (mooring ~) | ロープ | rōpu |
| knot (bowline, etc.) | 結び目 | musubime |

| deckrails | 手摺 | tesuri |
| gangway | 舷門 | genmon |

anchor	錨 [いかり]	ikari
to weigh anchor	錨をあげる	ikari wo ageru
to drop anchor	錨を下ろす	ikari wo orosu
anchor chain	錨鎖	byōsa

port (harbor)	港	minato
quay, wharf	埠頭	futō
to berth (moor)	係留する	keiryū suru
to cast off	出航する	shukkō suru

trip, voyage	旅行	ryokō
cruise (sea trip)	クルーズ	kurūzu
course (route)	針路	shinro
route (itinerary)	船のルート	fune no rūto

fairway	航路	kōro
shallows	浅瀬	asase
to run aground	浅瀬に乗り上げる	asase ni noriageru

storm	嵐	arashi
signal	信号	shingō
to sink (vi)	沈没する	chinbotsu suru
Man overboard!	落水したぞ！	ochimizu shi ta zo!
SOS (distress signal)	ＳＯＳ	esuōesu
ring buoy	救命浮輪	kyūmei ukiwa

T&P BOOKS

CITY

T&P Books Publishing

bus	バス	basu
streetcar	路面電車	romen densha
trolley bus	トロリーバス	tororībasu
route (of bus, etc.)	路線	rosen
number (e.g., bus ~)	番号	bangō
to go by ...	…で行く	… de iku
to get on (~ the bus)	乗る	noru
to get off ...	降りる	oriru
stop (e.g., bus ~)	停	toma
next stop	次の停車駅	tsugi no teishaeki
terminus	終着駅	shūchakueki
schedule	時刻表	jikoku hyō
to wait (vt)	待つ	matsu
ticket	乗車券	jōsha ken
fare	運賃	unchin
cashier (ticket seller)	販売員	hanbai in
ticket inspection	集札	shū satsu
ticket inspector	車掌	shashō
to be late (for ...)	遅れる	okureru
to miss (~ the train, etc.)	逃す	nogasu
to be in a hurry	急ぐ	isogu
taxi, cab	タクシー	takushī
taxi driver	タクシーの運転手	takushī no unten shu
by taxi	タクシーで	takushī de
taxi stand	タクシー乗り場	takushī noriba
to call a taxi	タクシーを呼ぶ	takushī wo yobu
to take a taxi	タクシーに乗る	takushī ni noru
traffic	交通	kōtsū
traffic jam	渋滞	jūtai
rush hour	ラッシュアワー	rasshuawā
to park (vi)	駐車する	chūsha suru
to park (vt)	駐車する	chūsha suru
parking lot	駐車場	chūsha jō
subway	地下鉄	chikatetsu
station	駅	eki
to take the subway	地下鉄で行く	chikatetsu de iku

| train | 列車 | ressha |
| train station | 鉄道駅 | tetsudō eki |

28. City. Life in the city

city, town	市、町	shi, machi
capital city	首都	shuto
village	村	mura

city map	市街地図	shigai chizu
downtown	中心街	chūshin gai
suburb	郊外	kōgai
suburban (adj)	郊外の	kōgai no

outskirts	町外れ	machihazure
environs (suburbs)	近郊	kinkō
city block	街区	gaiku
residential block (area)	住宅街	jūtaku gai

traffic	交通	kōtsū
traffic lights	信号	shingō
public transportation	公共交通機関	kōkyō kōtsū kikan
intersection	交差点	kōsaten

crosswalk	横断歩道	ōdan hodō
pedestrian underpass	地下道	chikadō
to cross (~ the street)	横断する	ōdan suru
pedestrian	歩行者	hokō sha
sidewalk	歩道	hodō

bridge	橋	hashi
embankment (river walk)	堤防	teibō
fountain	噴水	funsui

allée (garden walkway)	散歩道	sanpomichi
park	公園	kōen
boulevard	大通り	ōdōri
square	広場	hiroba
avenue (wide street)	アヴェニュー	avenyū
street	通り	tōri
side street	わき道 [脇道]	wakimichi
dead end	行き止まり	ikidomari

house	家屋	kaoku
building	建物	tatemono
skyscraper	摩天楼	matenrō

facade	ファサード	fasādo
roof	屋根	yane
window	窓	mado

arch	アーチ	āchi
column	柱	hashira
corner	角	kado

store window	ショーウインドー	shōuindō
signboard (store sign, etc.)	店看板	mise kanban
poster	ポスター	posutā
advertising poster	広告ポスター	kōkoku posutā
billboard	広告掲示板	kōkoku keijiban

garbage, trash	ゴミ［ごみ］	gomi
trashcan (public ~)	ゴミ入れ	gomi ire
to litter (vi)	ゴミを投げ捨てる	gomi wo nagesuteru
garbage dump	ゴミ捨て場	gomi suteba

phone booth	電話ボックス	denwa bokkusu
lamppost	街灯柱	gaitō bashira
bench (park ~)	ベンチ	benchi

police officer	警官	keikan
police	警察	keisatsu
beggar	こじき	kojiki
homeless (n)	ホームレス	hōmuresu

29. Urban institutions

store	店、…屋	mise, …ya
drugstore, pharmacy	薬局	yakkyoku
eyeglass store	眼鏡店	megane ten
shopping mall	ショッピングモール	shoppingu mōru
supermarket	スーパーマーケット	sūpāmāketto

bakery	パン屋	panya
baker	パン職人	pan shokunin
candy store	菓子店	kashi ten
grocery store	食料品店	shokuryō hin ten
butcher shop	肉屋	nikuya

| produce store | 八百屋 | yaoya |
| market | 市場 | ichiba |

coffee house	喫茶店	kissaten
restaurant	レストラン	resutoran
pub, bar	パブ	pabu
pizzeria	ピザ屋	piza ya

hair salon	美容院	biyō in
post office	郵便局	yūbin kyoku
dry cleaners	クリーニング屋	kurīningu ya
photo studio	写真館	shashin kan

shoe store	靴屋	kutsuya
bookstore	本屋	honya
sporting goods store	スポーツ店	supōtsu ten
clothes repair shop	洋服直し専門店	yōfuku naoshi senmon ten
formal wear rental	貸衣裳店	kashi ishō ten
video rental store	レンタルビデオ店	rentarubideo ten
circus	サーカス	sākasu
zoo	動物園	dōbutsu en
movie theater	映画館	eiga kan
museum	博物館	hakubutsukan
library	図書館	toshokan
theater	劇場	gekijō
opera (opera house)	オペラハウス	opera hausu
nightclub	ナイトクラブ	naito kurabu
casino	カジノ	kajino
mosque	モスク	mosuku
synagogue	シナゴーグ	shinagōgu
cathedral	大聖堂	dai seidō
temple	寺院	jīn
church	教会	kyōkai
college	大学	daigaku
university	大学	daigaku
school	学校	gakkō
prefecture	県庁舎	ken chōsha
city hall	市役所	shiyaku sho
hotel	ホテル	hoteru
bank	銀行	ginkō
embassy	大使館	taishikan
travel agency	旅行代理店	ryokō dairi ten
information office	案内所	annai sho
currency exchange	両替所	ryōgae sho
subway	地下鉄	chikatetsu
hospital	病院	byōin
gas station	ガソリンスタンド	gasorin sutando
parking lot	駐車場	chūsha jō

30. Signs

signboard (store sign, etc.)	店看板	mise kanban
notice (door sign, etc.)	看板	kanban
poster	ポスター	posutā

direction sign	方向看板	hōkō kanban
arrow (sign)	矢印	yajirushi
caution	注意	chūi
warning sign	警告表示	keikoku hyōji
to warn (vt)	警告する	keikoku suru
rest day (weekly ~)	定休日	teikyū bi
timetable (schedule)	営業時間の看板	eigyō jikan no kanban
opening hours	営業時間	eigyō jikan
WELCOME!	ようこそ	yōkoso
ENTRANCE	入口	iriguchi
EXIT	出口	deguchi
PUSH	押す	osu
PULL	引く	hiku
OPEN	営業中	eigyō chū
CLOSED	休業日	kyūgyōbi
WOMEN	女性	josei
MEN	男性	dansei
DISCOUNTS	割引	waribiki
SALE	バーゲンセール	bāgen sēru
NEW!	新発売！	shin hatsubai!
FREE	無料	muryō
ATTENTION!	ご注意！	go chūi!
NO VACANCIES	満室	manshitsu
RESERVED	御予約席	go yoyaku seki
ADMINISTRATION	支配人	shihainin
STAFF ONLY	関係者以外立入禁止	kankei sha igai tachīrikinshi
BEWARE OF THE DOG!	猛犬注意	mōken chūi
NO SMOKING	禁煙	kinen
DO NOT TOUCH!	手を触れるな	te wo fureru na
DANGEROUS	危険	kiken
DANGER	危険	kiken
HIGH VOLTAGE	高電圧	kō denatsu
NO SWIMMING!	水泳禁止	suiei kinshi
OUT OF ORDER	故障中	koshō chū
FLAMMABLE	可燃性物質	kanen sei busshitsu
FORBIDDEN	禁止	kinshi
NO TRESPASSING!	通り抜け禁止	tōrinuke kinshi
WET PAINT	ペンキ塗りたて	penki nuritate

31. Shopping

to buy (purchase)	買う	kau
purchase	買い物	kaimono
to go shopping	買い物に行く	kaimono ni iku
shopping	ショッピング	shoppingu
to be open (ab. store)	開いている	hiraite iru
to be closed	閉まっている	shimatte iru
footwear, shoes	履物	hakimono
clothes, clothing	洋服	yōfuku
cosmetics	化粧品	keshō hin
food products	食料品	shokuryō hin
gift, present	土産	miyage
salesman	店員、売り子	tenin, uriko
saleswoman	店員、売り子	tenin, uriko
check out, cash desk	レジ	reji
mirror	鏡	kagami
counter (store ~)	カウンター	kauntā
fitting room	試着室	shichaku shitsu
to try on	試着する	shichaku suru
to fit (ab. dress, etc.)	合う	au
to like (I like ...)	好む	konomu
price	価格	kakaku
price tag	値札	nefuda
to cost (vt)	かかる	kakaru
How much?	いくら？	ikura ?
discount	割引	waribiki
inexpensive (adj)	安価な	anka na
cheap (adj)	安い	yasui
expensive (adj)	高い	takai
It's expensive	それは高い	sore wa takai
rental (n)	レンタル	rentaru
to rent (~ a tuxedo)	レンタルする	rentaru suru
credit (trade credit)	信用取引	shinyō torihiki
on credit (adv)	付けで	tsuke de

T&P BOOKS

CLOTHING & ACCESSORIES

T&P Books Publishing

32. Outerwear. Coats

clothes	洋服	yōfuku
outerwear	上着	uwagi
winter clothing	冬服	fuyu fuku

coat (overcoat)	オーバーコート	ōbā kōto
fur coat	毛皮のコート	kegawa no kōto
fur jacket	毛皮のジャケット	kegawa no jaketto
down coat	ダウンコート	daun kōto

jacket (e.g., leather ~)	ジャケット	jaketto
raincoat (trenchcoat, etc.)	レインコート	reinkōto
waterproof (adj)	防水の	bōsui no

33. Men's & women's clothing

shirt (button shirt)	ワイシャツ	waishatsu
pants	ズボン	zubon
jeans	ジーンズ	jīnzu
suit jacket	ジャケット	jaketto
suit	背広	sebiro

dress (frock)	ドレス	doresu
skirt	スカート	sukāto
blouse	ブラウス	burausu
knitted jacket (cardigan, etc.)	ニットジャケット	nitto jaketto
jacket (of woman's suit)	ジャケット	jaketto

T-shirt	Tシャツ	tīshatsu
shorts (short trousers)	半ズボン	han zubon
tracksuit	トラックスーツ	torakku sūtsu
bathrobe	バスローブ	basurōbu
pajamas	パジャマ	pajama

| sweater | セーター | sētā |
| pullover | プルオーバー | puruōbā |

vest	ベスト	besuto
tailcoat	燕尾服	enbifuku
tuxedo	タキシード	takishīdo
uniform	制服	seifuku
workwear	作業服	sagyō fuku

overalls	オーバーオール	ōbā ōru
coat (e.g., doctor's smock)	コート	kōto

34. Clothing. Underwear

underwear	下着	shitagi
boxers	ボクサーパンツ	bokusā pantsu
panties	パンティー	pantī
undershirt (A-shirt)	タンクトップ	tanku toppu
socks	靴下	kutsushita
nightgown	ネグリジェ	negurije
bra	ブラジャー	burajā
knee highs	ニーソックス	nīsokkusu
(knee-high socks)		
pantyhose	パンティストッキング	pantī sutokkingu
stockings (thigh highs)	ストッキング	sutokkingu
bathing suit	水着	mizugi

35. Headwear

hat	帽子	bōshi
fedora	フェドーラ帽	fedōra bō
baseball cap	野球帽	yakyū bō
flatcap	ハンチング帽	hanchingu bō
beret	ベレー帽	berē bō
hood	フード	fūdo
panama hat	パナマ帽	panama bō
knit cap (knitted hat)	ニット帽	nitto bō
headscarf	ヘッドスカーフ	heddo sukāfu
women's hat	婦人帽子	fujin bōshi
hard hat	安全ヘルメット	anzen herumetto
garrison cap	略帽	rya ku bō
helmet	ヘルメット	herumetto
derby	山高帽	yamataka bō
top hat	シルクハット	shiruku hatto

36. Footwear

footwear	靴	kutsu
shoes (men's shoes)	アンクルブーツ	ankuru būtsu
shoes (women's shoes)	パンプス	panpusu

boots (cowboy ~)	ブーツ	būtsu
slippers	スリッパ	surippa
tennis shoes (e.g., Nike ~)	テニスシューズ	tenisu shūzu
sneakers (e.g., Converse ~)	スニーカー	sunīkā
sandals	サンダル	sandaru
cobbler (shoe repairer)	靴修理屋	kutsu shūri ya
heel	かかと [踵]	kakato
pair (of shoes)	靴一足	kutsu issoku
shoestring	靴ひも	kutsu himo
to lace (vt)	靴ひもを結ぶ	kutsu himo wo musubu
shoehorn	靴べら	kutsubera
shoe polish	靴クリーム	kutsu kurīmu

37. Personal accessories

gloves	手袋	tebukuro
mittens	ミトン	miton
scarf (muffler)	マフラー	mafurā
glasses (eyeglasses)	めがね [眼鏡]	megane
frame (eyeglass ~)	めがねのふち	megane no fuchi
umbrella	傘	kasa
walking stick	杖	tsue
hairbrush	ヘアブラシ	hea burashi
fan	扇子	sensu
tie (necktie)	ネクタイ	nekutai
bow tie	蝶ネクタイ	chō nekutai
suspenders	サスペンダー	sasupendā
handkerchief	ハンカチ	hankachi
comb	くし [櫛]	kushi
barrette	髪留め	kami tome
hairpin	ヘアピン	hea pin
buckle	バックル	bakkuru
belt	ベルト	beruto
shoulder strap	ショルダーベルト	shorudā beruto
bag (handbag)	バッグ	baggu
purse	ハンドバッグ	hando baggu
backpack	バックパック	bakku pakku

38. Clothing. Miscellaneous

fashion	ファッション	fasshon
in vogue (adj)	流行の	ryūkō no
fashion designer	ファッションデザイナー	fasshon dezainā
collar	襟	eri
pocket	ポケット	poketto
pocket (as adj)	ポケットの	poketto no
sleeve	袖	sode
hanging loop	ハンガールーブ	hangā rūpu
fly (on trousers)	ズボンのファスナー	zubon no fasunā
zipper (fastener)	チャック	chakku
fastener	ファスナー	fasunā
button	ボタン	botan
buttonhole	ボタンの穴	botan no ana
to come off (ab. button)	取れる	toreru
to sew (vi, vt)	縫う	nū
to embroider (vi, vt)	刺繍する	shishū suru
embroidery	刺繍	shishū
sewing needle	縫い針	nui bari
thread	糸	ito
seam	縫い目	nuime
to get dirty (vi)	汚れる	yogoreru
stain (mark, spot)	染み	shimi
to crease, crumple (vi)	しわになる	shiwa ni naru
to tear, to rip (vt)	引き裂く	hikisaku
clothes moth	コイガ	koi ga

39. Personal care. Cosmetics

toothpaste	歯磨き粉	hamigakiko
toothbrush	歯ブラシ	haburashi
to brush one's teeth	歯を磨く	ha wo migaku
razor	カミソリ［剃刀］	kamisori
shaving cream	シェーピングクリーム	shēbingu kurīmu
to shave (vi)	ひげを剃る	hige wo soru
soap	せっけん［石鹸］	sekken
shampoo	シャンプー	shanpū
scissors	はさみ	hasami
nail file	爪やすり	tsume yasuri
nail clippers	爪切り	tsume giri
tweezers	ピンセット	pinsetto

cosmetics	化粧品	keshō hin
face mask	フェイスパック	feisu pakku
manicure	マニキュア	manikyua
to have a manicure	マニキュアをしてもらう	manikyua wo shi te morau
pedicure	ペディキュア	pedikyua

make-up bag	化粧ポーチ	keshō pōchi
face powder	フェイスパウダー	feisu pauda
powder compact	ファンデーション	fandēshon
blusher	チーク	chīku

perfume (bottled)	香水	kōsui
toilet water (perfume)	オードトワレ	ōdotoware
lotion	ローション	rō shon
cologne	オーデコロン	ōdekoron

eyeshadow	アイシャドウ	aishadō
eyeliner	アイライナー	airainā
mascara	マスカラ	masukara

lipstick	口紅	kuchibeni
nail polish, enamel	ネイルポリッシュ	neiru porisshu
hair spray	ヘアスプレー	hea supurē
deodorant	デオドラント	deodoranto

cream	クリーム	kurīmu
face cream	フェイスクリーム	feisu kurīmu
hand cream	ハンドクリーム	hando kurīmu
anti-wrinkle cream	しわ取りクリーム	shiwa tori kurīmu
day cream	昼用クリーム	hiruyō kurīmu
night cream	夜用クリーム	yoruyō kurīmu
day (as adj)	昼用…	hiruyō ...
night (as adj)	夜用…	yoruyō ...

tampon	タンポン	tanpon
toilet paper	トイレットペーパー	toiretto pēpā
hair dryer	ヘアドライヤー	hea doraiyā

40. Watches. Clocks

watch (wristwatch)	時計	tokei
dial	ダイヤル	daiyaru
hand (of clock, watch)	針	hari
metal watch band	金属ベルト	kinzoku beruto
watch strap	腕時計バンド	udedokei bando

battery	電池	denchi
to be dead (battery)	切れる	kireru
to change a battery	電池を交換する	denchi wo kōkan suru
to run fast	進んでいる	susundeiru

to run slow	遅れている	okureteiru
wall clock	掛け時計	kakedokei
hourglass	砂時計	sunadokei
sundial	日時計	hidokei
alarm clock	目覚まし時計	mezamashi dokei
watchmaker	時計職人	tokei shokunin
to repair (vt)	修理する	shūri suru

EVERYDAY EXPERIENCE

T&P Books Publishing

money	お金	okane
currency exchange	両替	ryōgae
exchange rate	為替レート	kawase rēto
ATM	ＡＴＭ	ētīemu
coin	コイン	koin
dollar	ドル	doru
euro	ユーロ	yūro
lira	リラ	rira
Deutschmark	ドイツマルク	doitsu maruku
franc	フラン	furan
pound sterling	スターリング・ポンド	sutāringu pondo
yen	円	en
debt	債務	saimu
debtor	債務者	saimu sha
to lend (money)	貸す	kasu
to borrow (vi, vt)	借りる	kariru
bank	銀行	ginkō
account	口座	kōza
to deposit (vt)	預金する	yokin suru
to deposit into the account	口座に預金する	kōza ni yokin suru
to withdraw (vt)	引き出す	hikidasu
credit card	クレジットカード	kurejitto kādo
cash	現金	genkin
check	小切手	kogitte
to write a check	小切手を書く	kogitte wo kaku
checkbook	小切手帳	kogitte chō
wallet	財布	saifu
change purse	小銭入れ	kozeni ire
billfold	札入れ	satsu ire
safe	金庫	kinko
heir	相続人	sōzokunin
inheritance	相続	sōzoku
fortune (wealth)	財産	zaisan
lease	賃貸	chintai
rent (money)	家賃	yachin
to rent (sth from sb)	借りる	kariru

price	価格	kakaku
cost	費用	hiyō
sum	合計金額	gōkei kingaku

to spend (vt)	お金を使う	okane wo tsukau
expenses	出費	shuppi
to economize (vi, vt)	倹約する	kenyaku suru
economical	節約の	setsuyaku no

to pay (vi, vt)	払う	harau
payment	支払い	shiharai
change (give the ~)	おつり	o tsuri

tax	税	zei
fine	罰金	bakkin
to fine (vt)	罰金を科す	bakkin wo kasu

42. Post. Postal service

post office	郵便局	yūbin kyoku
mail (letters, etc.)	郵便物	yūbin butsu
mailman	郵便配達人	yūbin haitatsu jin
opening hours	営業時間	eigyō jikan

letter	手紙	tegami
registered letter	書留郵便	kakitome yūbin
postcard	はがき［葉書］	hagaki
telegram	電報	denpō
package (parcel)	小包	kozutsumi
money transfer	送金	sōkin

to receive (vt)	受け取る	uketoru
to send (vt)	送る	okuru
sending	送信	sōshin

address	住所	jūsho
ZIP code	郵便番号	yūbin bangō
sender	送り主	okurinushi
receiver	受取人	uketorinin

| name (first name) | 名前 | namae |
| surname (last name) | 姓 | sei |

postage rate	郵便料金	yūbin ryōkin
standard (adj)	通常の	tsūjō no
economical (adj)	エコノミー航空	ekonomīkōkū

weight	重さ	omo sa
to weigh (~ letters)	量る	hakaru
envelope	封筒	fūtō

postage stamp	郵便切手	yūbin kitte
to stamp an envelope	封筒に切手を貼る	fūtō ni kitte wo haru

43. Banking

bank	銀行	ginkō
branch (of bank, etc.)	支店	shiten
bank clerk, consultant	銀行員	ginkōin
manager (director)	長	chō
bank account	口座	kōza
account number	口座番号	kōza bangō
checking account	当座預金口座	tōza yokin kōza
savings account	貯蓄預金口座	chochiku yokin kōza
to open an account	口座を開く	kōza wo hiraku
to close the account	口座を解約する	kōza wo kaiyaku suru
to deposit into the account	口座に預金する	kōza ni yokin suru
to withdraw (vt)	引き出す	hikidasu
deposit	預金	yokin
to make a deposit	預金する	yokin suru
wire transfer	送金	sōkin
to wire, to transfer	送金する	sōkin suru
sum	合計金額	gōkei kingaku
How much?	いくら？	ikura ?
signature	署名	shomei
to sign (vt)	署名する	shomei suru
credit card	クレジットカード	kurejitto kādo
code (PIN code)	コード	kōdo
credit card number	クレジットカード番号	kurejitto kādo bangō
ATM	ＡＴＭ	ētīemu
check	小切手	kogitte
to write a check	小切手を書く	kogitte wo kaku
checkbook	小切手帳	kogitte chō
loan (bank ~)	融資	yūshi
to apply for a loan	融資を申し込む	yūshi wo mōshikomu
to get a loan	融資を受ける	yūshi wo ukeru
to give a loan	融資を行う	yūshi wo okonau
guarantee	保障	hoshō

44. Telephone. Phone conversation

telephone	電話	denwa
mobile phone	携帯電話	keitai denwa
answering machine	留守番電話	rusuban denwa
to call (by phone)	電話する	denwa suru
phone call	電話	denwa
to dial a number	電話番号をダイアルする	denwa bangō wo daiaru suru
Hello!	もしもし	moshimoshi
to ask (vt)	問う	tō
to answer (vi, vt)	出る	deru
to hear (vt)	聞く	kiku
well (adv)	良く	yoku
not well (adv)	良くない	yoku nai
noises (interference)	電波障害	denpa shōgai
receiver	受話器	juwaki
to pick up (~ the phone)	電話に出る	denwa ni deru
to hang up (~ the phone)	電話を切る	denwa wo kiru
busy (adj)	話し中	hanashi chū
to ring (ab. phone)	鳴る	naru
telephone book	電話帳	denwa chō
local (adj)	市内の	shinai no
local call	市内電話	shinai denwa
long distance (~ call)	市外の	shigai no
long-distance call	市外電話	shigai denwa
international (adj)	国際の	kokusai no
international call	国際電話	kokusai denwa

45. Mobile telephone

mobile phone	携帯電話	keitai denwa
display	ディスプレイ	disupurei
button	ボタン	botan
SIM card	ＳＩＭカード	shimu kādo
battery	電池	denchi
to be dead (battery)	切れる	kireru
charger	充電器	jūden ki
menu	メニュー	menyū
settings	設定	settei
tune (melody)	メロディー	merodī

to select (vt)	選択する	sentaku suru
calculator	電卓	dentaku
voice mail	ボイスメール	boisu mēru
alarm clock	目覚まし	mezamashi
contacts	連絡先	renraku saki

| SMS (text message) | テキストメッセージ | tekisuto messēji |
| subscriber | 加入者 | kanyū sha |

46. Stationery

| ballpoint pen | ボールペン | bōrupen |
| fountain pen | 万年筆 | mannenhitsu |

pencil	鉛筆	enpitsu
highlighter	蛍光ペン	keikō pen
felt-tip pen	フェルトペン	feruto pen

| notepad | メモ帳 | memo chō |
| agenda (diary) | 手帳 | techō |

ruler	定規	jōgi
calculator	電卓	dentaku
eraser	消しゴム	keshigomu
thumbtack	画鋲	gabyō
paper clip	ゼムクリップ	zemu kurippu

glue	糊	nori
stapler	ホッチキス	hocchikisu
hole punch	パンチ	panchi
pencil sharpener	鉛筆削り	enpitsu kezuri

47. Foreign languages

language	言語	gengo
foreign (adj)	外国の	gaikoku no
foreign language	外国語	gaikoku go
to study (vt)	勉強する	benkyō suru
to learn (language, etc.)	学ぶ	manabu

to read (vi, vt)	読む	yomu
to speak (vi, vt)	話す	hanasu
to understand (vt)	理解する	rikai suru
to write (vt)	書く	kaku

fast (adv)	速く	hayaku
slowly (adv)	ゆっくり	yukkuri
fluently (adv)	流ちょうに	ryūchō ni

rules	規則	kisoku
grammar	文法	bunpō
vocabulary	語彙	goi
phonetics	音声学	onseigaku

textbook	教科書	kyōkasho
dictionary	辞書	jisho
teach-yourself book	独習書	dokushū sho
phrasebook	慣用表現集	kanyō hyōgen shū

cassette	カセットテープ	kasettotēpu
videotape	ビデオテープ	bideotēpu
CD, compact disc	ＣＤ（シーディー）	shīdī
DVD	ＤＶＤ ［ディーブイディー］	dībuidī

alphabet	アルファベット	arufabetto
to spell (vt)	スペリングを言う	superingu wo iu
pronunciation	発音	hatsuon

accent	なまり［訛り］	namari
with an accent	訛りのある	namari no aru
without an accent	訛りのない	namari no nai

| word | 単語 | tango |
| meaning | 意味 | imi |

course (e.g., a French ~)	講座	kōza
to sign up	申し込む	mōshikomu
teacher	先生	sensei

translation (process)	翻訳	honyaku
translation (text, etc.)	訳文	yakubun
translator	翻訳者	honyaku sha
interpreter	通訳者	tsūyaku sha

| polyglot | ポリグロット | porigurotto |
| memory | 記憶 | kioku |

T&P BOOKS

MEALS. RESTAURANT

T&P Books Publishing

48. Table setting

spoon	スプーン	supūn
knife	ナイフ	naifu
fork	フォーク	fōku
cup (e.g., coffee ~)	カップ	kappu
plate (dinner ~)	皿	sara
saucer	ソーサー	sōsā
napkin (on table)	ナフキン	nafukin
toothpick	つまようじ [爪楊枝]	tsumayōji

49. Restaurant

restaurant	レストラン	resutoran
coffee house	喫茶店	kissaten
pub, bar	パブ、バー	pabu, bā
tearoom	喫茶店	kissaten
waiter	ウェイター	weitā
waitress	ウェートレス	wētoresu
bartender	バーテンダー	bātendā
menu	メニュー	menyū
wine list	ワインリスト	wain risuto
to book a table	テーブルを予約する	tēburu wo yoyaku suru
course, dish	料理	ryōri
to order (meal)	注文する	chūmon suru
to make an order	注文する	chūmon suru
aperitif	アペリティフ	aperitifu
appetizer	前菜	zensai
dessert	デザート	dezāto
check	お勘定	okanjō
to pay the check	勘定を払う	kanjō wo harau
to give change	釣り銭を渡す	tsurisen wo watasu
tip	チップ	chippu

50. Meals

food	食べ物	tabemono
to eat (vi, vt)	食べる	taberu

breakfast	朝食	chōshoku
to have breakfast	朝食をとる	chōshoku wo toru
lunch	昼食	chūshoku
to have lunch	昼食をとる	chūshoku wo toru
dinner	夕食	yūshoku
to have dinner	夕食をとる	yūshoku wo toru

| appetite | 食欲 | shokuyoku |
| Enjoy your meal! | どうぞお召し上がり 下さい！ | dōzo o meshiagarikudasai! |

to open (~ a bottle)	開ける	akeru
to spill (liquid)	こぼす	kobosu
to spill out (vi)	こぼれる	koboreru

to boil (vi)	沸く	waku
to boil (vt)	沸かす	wakasu
boiled (~ water)	沸騰させた	futtō sase ta
to chill, cool down (vt)	冷やす	hiyasu
to chill (vi)	冷える	hieru

| taste, flavor | 味 | aji |
| aftertaste | 後味 | atoaji |

to slim down (lose weight)	ダイエットをする	daietto wo suru
diet	ダイエット	daietto
vitamin	ビタミン	bitamin
calorie	カロリー	karorī
vegetarian (n)	ベジタリアン	bejitarian
vegetarian (adj)	ベジタリアン用の	bejitarian yōno

fats (nutrient)	脂肪	shibō
proteins	タンパク質 [蛋白質]	tanpaku shitsu
carbohydrates	炭水化物	tansuikabutsu
slice (of lemon, ham)	スライス	suraisu
piece (of cake, pie)	一切れ	ichi kire
crumb (of bread, cake, etc.)	くず	kuzu

51. Cooked dishes

course, dish	料理	ryōri
cuisine	料理	ryōri
recipe	レシピ	reshipi
portion	一人前	ichi ninmae

salad	サラダ	sarada
soup	スープ	sūpu
clear soup (broth)	ブイヨン	buiyon
sandwich (bread)	サンドイッチ	sandoicchi

fried eggs	目玉焼き	medamayaki
fried meatballs	クロケット	kuroketto
hamburger (beefburger)	ハンバーガー	hanbāgā
beefsteak	ビーフステーキ	bīfusutēki
stew	シチュー	shichū
side dish	付け合わせ	tsukeawase
spaghetti	スパゲッティ	supagetti
mashed potatoes	マッシュポテト	masshupoteto
pizza	ピザ	piza
porridge (oatmeal, etc.)	ポリッジ	porijji
omelet	オムレツ	omuretsu
boiled (e.g., ~ beef)	煮た	ni ta
smoked (adj)	薫製の	kunsei no
fried (adj)	揚げた	age ta
dried (adj)	干した	hoshi ta
frozen (adj)	冷凍の	reitō no
pickled (adj)	酢漬けの	suzuke no
sweet (sugary)	甘い	amai
salty (adj)	塩味の	shioaji no
cold (adj)	冷たい	tsumetai
hot (adj)	熱い	atsui
bitter (adj)	苦い	nigai
tasty (adj)	美味しい	oishī
to cook in boiling water	水で煮る	mizu de niru
to cook (dinner)	料理をする	ryōri wo suru
to fry (vt)	揚げる	ageru
to heat up (food)	温める	atatameru
to salt (vt)	塩をかける	shio wo kakeru
to pepper (vt)	コショウをかける	koshō wo kakeru
to grate (vt)	すりおろす	suri orosu
peel (n)	皮	kawa
to peel (vt)	皮をむく	kawa wo muku

52. Food

meat	肉	niku
chicken	鶏	niwatori
Rock Cornish hen (poussin)	若鶏	wakadori
duck	ダック	dakku
goose	ガチョウ	gachō
game	獲物	emono
turkey	七面鳥	shichimenchuō
pork	豚肉	buta niku
veal	子牛肉	kōshi niku

lamb	子羊肉	kohitsuji niku
beef	牛肉	gyū niku
rabbit	兎肉	usagi niku

sausage (bologna, pepperoni, etc.)	ソーセージ	sōsēji
vienna sausage (frankfurter)	ソーセージ	sōsēji
bacon	ベーコン	bēkon
ham	ハム	hamu
gammon	ガモン	gamon

pâté	パテ	pate
liver	レバー	rebā
lard	ラード	rādo
hamburger (ground beef)	挽肉	hikiniku
tongue	タン	tan

egg	卵	tamago
eggs	卵	tamago
egg white	卵の白身	tamago no shiromi
egg yolk	卵の黄身	tamago no kimi

fish	魚	sakana
seafood	魚介	gyokai
caviar	キャビア	kyabia

crab	カニ [蟹]	kani
shrimp	エビ	ebi
oyster	カキ [牡蠣]	kaki
spiny lobster	伊勢エビ	ise ebi
octopus	タコ	tako
squid	イカ	ika

sturgeon	チョウザメ	chōzame
salmon	サケ [鮭]	sake
halibut	ハリバット	haribatto

cod	タラ [鱈]	tara
mackerel	サバ [鯖]	saba
tuna	マグロ [鮪]	maguro
eel	ウナギ [鰻]	unagi

trout	マス [鱒]	masu
sardine	イワシ	iwashi
pike	カワカマス	kawakamasu
herring	ニシン	nishin

bread	パン	pan
cheese	チーズ	chīzu
sugar	砂糖	satō
salt	塩	shio

rice	米	kome
pasta	パスタ	pasuta
noodles	麺	men
butter	バター	batā
vegetable oil	植物油	shokubutsu yu
sunflower oil	ひまわり油	himawari yu
margarine	マーガリン	māgarin
olives	オリーブ	orību
olive oil	オリーブ油	orību yu
milk	乳、ミルク	nyū, miruku
condensed milk	練乳	rennyū
yogurt	ヨーグルト	yōguruto
sour cream	サワークリーム	sawā kurīmu
cream (of milk)	クリーム	kurīmu
mayonnaise	マヨネーズ	mayonēzu
buttercream	バタークリーム	batā kurīmu
cereal grains (wheat, etc.)	穀物	kokumotsu
flour	小麦粉	komugiko
canned food	缶詰	kanzume
cornflakes	コーンフレーク	kōn furēku
honey	蜂蜜	hachimitsu
jam	ジャム	jamu
chewing gum	チューインガム	chūin gamu

53. Drinks

water	水	mizu
drinking water	飲用水	inyō sui
mineral water	ミネラルウォーター	mineraru wōtā
still (adj)	無炭酸の	mu tansan no
carbonated (adj)	炭酸の	tansan no
sparkling (adj)	発泡性の	happō sei no
ice	氷	kōri
with ice	氷入りの	kōri iri no
non-alcoholic (adj)	ノンアルコールの	non arukōru no
soft drink	炭酸飲料	tansan inryō
refreshing drink	清涼飲料水	seiryōinryōsui
lemonade	レモネード	remonēdo
liquors	アルコール	arukōru
wine	ワイン	wain
white wine	白ワイン	shiro wain

red wine	赤ワイン	aka wain
liqueur	リキュール	rikyūru
champagne	シャンパン	shanpan
vermouth	ベルモット	berumotto
whisky	ウイスキー	uisukī
vodka	ウォッカ	wokka
gin	ジン	jin
cognac	コニャック	konyakku
rum	ラム酒	ramu shu
coffee	コーヒー	kōhī
black coffee	ブラックコーヒー	burakku kōhī
coffee with milk	ミルク入りコーヒー	miruku iri kōhī
cappuccino	カプチーノ	kapuchīno
instant coffee	インスタントコーヒー	insutanto kōhī
milk	乳、ミルク	nyū, miruku
cocktail	カクテル	kakuteru
milkshake	ミルクセーキ	miruku sēki
juice	ジュース	jūsu
tomato juice	トマトジュース	tomato jūsu
orange juice	オレンジジュース	orenji jūsu
freshly squeezed juice	搾りたてのジュース	shibori tate no jūsu
beer	ビール	bīru
light beer	ライトビール	raito bīru
dark beer	黒ビール	kuro bīru
tea	茶	cha
black tea	紅茶	kō cha
green tea	緑茶	ryoku cha

54. Vegetables

vegetables	野菜	yasai
greens	青物	aomono
tomato	トマト	tomato
cucumber	きゅうり [胡瓜]	kyūri
carrot	ニンジン [人参]	ninjin
potato	ジャガイモ	jagaimo
onion	たまねぎ [玉葱]	tamanegi
garlic	ニンニク	ninniku
cabbage	キャベツ	kyabetsu
cauliflower	カリフラワー	karifurawā
Brussels sprouts	メキャベツ	mekyabetsu
broccoli	ブロッコリー	burokkorī

beetroot	テーブルビート	tēburu bīto
eggplant	ナス	nasu
zucchini	ズッキーニ	zukkīni
pumpkin	カボチャ	kabocha
turnip	カブ	kabu
parsley	パセリ	paseri
dill	ディル	diru
lettuce	レタス	retasu
celery	セロリ	serori
asparagus	アスパラガス	asuparagasu
spinach	ホウレンソウ	hōrensō
pea	エンドウ	endō
beans	豆類	mamerui
corn (maize)	トウモロコシ	tōmorokoshi
kidney bean	金時豆	kintoki mame
bell pepper	コショウ	koshō
radish	ハツカダイコン	hatsukadaikon
artichoke	アーティチョーク	ātichōku

55. Fruits. Nuts

fruit	果物	kudamono
apple	リンゴ	ringo
pear	洋梨	yōnashi
lemon	レモン	remon
orange	オレンジ	orenji
strawberry	イチゴ（苺）	ichigo
mandarin	マンダリン	mandarin
plum	プラム	puramu
peach	モモ［桃］	momo
apricot	アンズ［杏子］	anzu
raspberry	ラズベリー（木苺）	razuberī
pineapple	パイナップル	painappuru
banana	バナナ	banana
watermelon	スイカ	suika
grape	ブドウ［葡萄］	budō
cherry	チェリー	cherī
sour cherry	サワー チェリー	sawā cherī
sweet cherry	スイート チェリー	suīto cherī
melon	メロン	meron
grapefruit	グレープフルーツ	gurēbu furūtsu
avocado	アボカド	abokado
papaya	パパイヤ	papaiya
mango	マンゴー	mangō

pomegranate	ザクロ	zakuro
redcurrant	フサスグリ	fusa suguri
blackcurrant	クロスグリ	kuro suguri
gooseberry	セイヨウスグリ	seiyō suguri
bilberry	ビルベリー	biruberī
blackberry	ブラックベリー	burakku berī
raisin	レーズン	rēzun
fig	イチジク	ichijiku
date	デーツ	dētsu
peanut	ピーナッツ	pīnattsu
almond	アーモンド	āmondo
walnut	クルミ（胡桃）	kurumi
hazelnut	ヘーゼルナッツ	hēzeru nattsu
coconut	ココナッツ	koko nattsu
pistachios	ピスタチオ	pisutachio

56. Bread. Candy

bakers' confectionery (pastry)	菓子類	kashi rui
bread	パン	pan
cookies	クッキー	kukkī
chocolate (n)	チョコレート	chokorēto
chocolate (as adj)	チョコレートの	chokorēto no
candy	キャンディー	kyandī
cake (e.g., cupcake)	ケーキ	kēki
cake (e.g., birthday ~)	ケーキ	kēki
pie (e.g., apple ~)	パイ	pai
filling (for cake, pie)	フィリング	firingu
whole fruit jam	ジャム	jamu
marmalade	マーマレード	māmarēdo
waffles	ワッフル	waffuru
ice-cream	アイスクリーム	aisukurīmu
pudding	プディング	pudingu

57. Spices

salt	塩	shio
salty (adj)	塩味の	shioaji no
to salt (vt)	塩をかける	shio wo kakeru
black pepper	黒コショウ	kuro koshō
red pepper (milled ~)	赤唐辛子	aka tōgarashi

mustard	マスタード	masutādo
horseradish	セイヨウワサビ	seiyō wasabi
condiment	調味料	chōmiryō
spice	香辛料	kōshinryō
sauce	ソース	sōsu
vinegar	酢、ビネガー	su, binegā
anise	アニス	anisu
basil	バジル	bajiru
cloves	クローブ	kurōbu
ginger	生姜、ジンジャー	shōga, jinjā
coriander	コリアンダー	koriandā
cinnamon	シナモン	shinamon
sesame	ゴマ [胡麻]	goma
bay leaf	ローリエ	rōrie
paprika	パプリカ	papurika
caraway	キャラウェイ	kyarawei
saffron	サフラン	safuran

PERSONAL
INFORMATION. FAMILY

T&P Books Publishing

58. Personal information. Forms

name (first name)	名前	namae
surname (last name)	姓	sei
date of birth	誕生日	tanjō bi
place of birth	出生地	shusseichi
nationality	国籍	kokuseki
place of residence	住所	jūsho
country	国	kuni
profession (occupation)	職業	shokugyō
gender, sex	性	sei
height	身長	shinchō
weight	体重	taijū

59. Family members. Relatives

mother	母親	hahaoya
father	父親	chichioya
son	息子	musuko
daughter	娘	musume
younger daughter	下の娘	shitano musume
younger son	下の息子	shitano musuko
eldest daughter	長女	chōjo
eldest son	長男	chōnan
brother	兄、弟、兄弟	ani, otōto, kyoōdai
elder brother	兄	ani
younger brother	弟	otōto
sister	姉、妹、姉妹	ane, imōto, shimai
elder sister	姉	ane
younger sister	妹	imōto
cousin (masc.)	従兄弟	itoko
cousin (fem.)	従姉妹	itoko
mom, mommy	お母さん	okāsan
dad, daddy	お父さん	otōsan
parents	親	oya
child	子供	kodomo
children	子供	kodomo
grandmother	祖母	sobo
grandfather	祖父	sofu

grandson	孫息子	mago musuko
granddaughter	孫娘	mago musume
grandchildren	孫	mago

uncle	伯父	oji
aunt	伯母	oba
nephew	甥	oi
niece	姪	mei

mother-in-law (wife's mother)	妻の母親	tsuma no hahaoya
father-in-law (husband's father)	義父	gifu
son-in-law (daughter's husband)	娘の夫	musume no otto
stepmother	継母	keibo
stepfather	継父	keifu

infant	乳児	nyūji
baby (infant)	赤ん坊	akanbō
little boy, kid	子供	kodomo

wife	妻	tsuma
husband	夫	otto
spouse (husband)	配偶者	haigū sha
spouse (wife)	配偶者	haigū sha

married (masc.)	既婚の	kikon no
married (fem.)	既婚の	kikon no
single (unmarried)	独身の	dokushin no
bachelor	独身男性	dokushin dansei
divorced (masc.)	離婚した	rikon shi ta
widow	未亡人	mibōjin
widower	男やもめ	otokoyamome

relative	親戚	shinseki
close relative	近い親戚	chikai shinseki
distant relative	遠い親戚	tōi shinseki
relatives	親族	shinzoku

orphan (boy or girl)	孤児	koji
guardian (of minor)	後見人	kōkennin
to adopt (a boy)	養子にする	yōshi ni suru
to adopt (a girl)	養女にする	yōjo ni suru

60. Friends. Coworkers

friend (masc.)	友達	tomodachi
friend (fem.)	友達	tomodachi
friendship	友情	yūjō

to be friends	友達だ	tomodachi da
buddy (masc.)	友達	tomodachi
buddy (fem.)	女友達	onna tomodachi
partner	パートナー	pātonā
chief (boss)	長	chō
superior (n)	上司、上役	jōshi, uwayaku
owner, proprietor	経営者	keieisha
subordinate (n)	部下	buka
colleague	同僚	dōryō
acquaintance (person)	知り合い	shiriai
fellow traveler	同調者	dōchō sha
classmate	クラスメート	kurasumēto
neighbor (masc.)	隣人、近所	rinjin, kinjo
neighbor (fem.)	隣人、近所	rinjin, kinjo
neighbors	隣人	rinjin

HUMAN BODY. MEDICINE

T&P Books Publishing

61. Head

head	頭	atama
face	顔	kao
nose	鼻	hana
mouth	口	kuchi
eye	眼	me
eyes	両眼	ryōgan
pupil	瞳	hitomi
eyebrow	眉	mayu
eyelash	まつげ	matsuge
eyelid	まぶた	mabuta
tongue	舌	shita
tooth	歯	ha
lips	唇	kuchibiru
cheekbones	頬骨	hōbone
gum	歯茎	haguki
palate	口蓋	kōgai
nostrils	鼻孔	bikō
chin	あご（頤）	ago
jaw	顎	ago
cheek	頬	hō
forehead	額	hitai
temple	こめかみ	komekami
ear	耳	mimi
back of the head	後頭部	kōtōbu
neck	首	kubi
throat	喉	nodo
hair	髪の毛	kaminoke
hairstyle	髪形	kamigata
haircut	髪型	kamigata
wig	かつら	katsura
mustache	口ひげ	kuchihige
beard	あごひげ	agohige
to have (a beard, etc.)	生やしている	hayashi te iru
braid	三つ編み	mitsu ami
sideburns	もみあげ	momiage
red-haired (adj)	赤毛の	akage no
gray (hair)	白髪の	hakuhatsu no

bald (adj)	はげ頭の	hageatama no
bald patch	はげた部分	hage ta bubun
ponytail	ポニーテール	ponītēru
bangs	前髪	maegami

62. Human body

hand	手	te
arm	腕	ude
finger	指	yubi
toe	つま先	tsumasaki
thumb	親指	oyayubi
little finger	小指	koyubi
nail	爪	tsume
fist	拳	kobushi
palm	手のひら	tenohira
wrist	手首	tekubi
forearm	前腕	zen wan
elbow	肘	hiji
shoulder	肩	kata
leg	足 [脚]	ashi
foot	足	ashi
knee	膝	hiza
calf (part of leg)	ふくらはぎ	fuku ra hagi
hip	腰	koshi
heel	かかと [踵]	kakato
body	身体	shintai
stomach	腹	hara
chest	胸	mune
breast	乳房	chibusa
flank	脇腹	wakibara
back	背中	senaka
lower back	腰背部	yōwa ibu
waist	腰	koshi
navel (belly button)	へそ [臍]	heso
buttocks	臀部	denbu
bottom	尻	shiri
beauty mark	美人ぼくろ	bijinbokuro
birthmark (café au lait spot)	母斑	bohan
tattoo	タトゥー	tatū
scar	傷跡	kizuato

63. Diseases

sickness	病気	byōki
to be sick	病気になる	byōki ni naru
health	健康	kenkō
runny nose (coryza)	鼻水	hanamizu
tonsillitis	狭心症	kyōshinshō
cold (illness)	風邪	kaze
to catch a cold	風邪をひく	kaze wo hiku
bronchitis	気管支炎	kikanshien
pneumonia	肺炎	haien
flu, influenza	インフルエンザ	infuruenza
nearsighted (adj)	近視の	kinshi no
farsighted (adj)	遠視の	enshi no
strabismus (crossed eyes)	斜視	shashi
cross-eyed (adj)	斜視の	shashi no
cataract	白内障	hakunaishō
glaucoma	緑内障	ryokunaishō
stroke	脳卒中	nōsocchū
heart attack	心臓発作	shinzō hossa
myocardial infarction	心筋梗塞	shinkinkōsoku
paralysis	まひ［麻痺］	mahi
to paralyze (vt)	まひさせる	mahi saseru
allergy	アレルギー	arerugī
asthma	ぜんそく［喘息］	zensoku
diabetes	糖尿病	tōnyō byō
toothache	歯痛	shitsū
caries	カリエス	kariesu
diarrhea	下痢	geri
constipation	便秘	benpi
stomach upset	胃のむかつき	i no mukatsuki
food poisoning	食中毒	shokuchūdoku
to get food poisoning	食中毒にかかる	shokuchūdoku ni kakaru
arthritis	関節炎	kansetsu en
rickets	くる病	kuru yamai
rheumatism	リューマチ	ryūmachi
atherosclerosis	アテローム性動脈硬化	ate rōmu sei dōmyaku kōka
gastritis	胃炎	ien
appendicitis	虫垂炎	chūsuien
cholecystitis	胆嚢炎	tannō en
ulcer	潰瘍	kaiyō

measles	麻疹	hashika
rubella (German measles)	風疹	fūshin
jaundice	黄疸	ōdan
hepatitis	肝炎	kanen
schizophrenia	統合失調症	tōgō shicchō shō
rabies (hydrophobia)	恐水病	kyōsuibyō
neurosis	神経症	shinkeishō
concussion	脳震とう（脳震盪）	nōshintō
cancer	がん［癌］	gan
sclerosis	硬化症	kōka shō
multiple sclerosis	多発性硬化症	tahatsu sei kōka shō
alcoholism	アルコール依存症	arukōru izon shō
alcoholic (n)	アルコール依存症患者	arukōru izon shō kanja
syphilis	梅毒	baidoku
AIDS	エイズ	eizu
tumor	腫瘍	shuyō
malignant (adj)	悪性の	akusei no
benign (adj)	良性の	ryōsei no
fever	発熱	hatsunetsu
malaria	マラリア	mararia
gangrene	壊疽	eso
seasickness	船酔い	fune yoi
epilepsy	てんかん［癲癇］	tenkan
epidemic	伝染病	densen byō
typhus	チフス	chifusu
tuberculosis	結核	kekkaku
cholera	コレラ	korera
plague (bubonic ~)	ペスト	pesuto

64. Symptoms. Treatments. Part 1

symptom	兆候	chōkō
temperature	体温	taion
high temperature (fever)	熱	netsu
pulse	脈拍	myakuhaku
dizziness (vertigo)	目まい［眩暈］	memai
hot (adj)	熱い	atsui
shivering	震え	furue
pale (e.g., ~ face)	青白い	aojiroi
cough	咳	seki
to cough (vi)	咳をする	seki wo suru
to sneeze (vi)	くしゃみをする	kushami wo suru

faint	気絶	kizetsu
to faint (vi)	気絶する	kizetsu suru
bruise (hématome)	打ち身	uchimi
bump (lump)	たんこぶ	tankobu
to bang (bump)	あざができる	aza ga dekiru
contusion (bruise)	打撲傷	dabokushō
to get a bruise	打撲する	daboku suru
to limp (vi)	足を引きずる	ashi wo hikizuru
dislocation	脱臼	dakkyū
to dislocate (vt)	脱臼する	dakkyū suru
fracture	骨折	kossetsu
to have a fracture	骨折する	kossetsu suru
cut (e.g., paper ~)	切り傷	kirikizu
to cut oneself	切り傷を負う	kirikizu wo ō
bleeding	出血	shukketsu
burn (injury)	火傷	yakedo
to get burned	火傷する	yakedo suru
to prick (vt)	刺す	sasu
to prick oneself	自分を刺す	jibun wo sasu
to injure (vt)	けがする	kega suru
injury	けが [怪我]	kega
wound	負傷	fushō
trauma	外傷	gaishō
to be delirious	熱に浮かされる	netsu ni ukasareru
to stutter (vi)	どもる	domoru
sunstroke	日射病	nisshabyō

65. Symptoms. Treatments. Part 2

pain	痛み	itami
splinter (in foot, etc.)	とげ [棘]	toge
sweat (perspiration)	汗	ase
to sweat (perspire)	汗をかく	ase wo kaku
vomiting	嘔吐	ōto
convulsions	けいれん [痙攣]	keiren
pregnant (adj)	妊娠している	ninshin shi te iru
to be born	生まれる	umareru
delivery, labor	分娩	bumben
to deliver (~ a baby)	分娩する	bumben suru
abortion	妊娠中絶	ninshin chūzetsu
breathing, respiration	呼吸	kokyū
in-breath (inhalation)	息を吸うこと	iki wo sū koto

out-breath (exhalation)	息を吐くこと	iki wo haku koto
to exhale (breathe out)	息を吐く	iki wo haku
to inhale (vi)	息を吸う	iki wo sū

disabled person	障害者	shōgai sha
cripple	身障者	shinshōsha
drug addict	麻薬中毒者	mayaku chūdoku sha

deaf (adj)	ろうの［聾の］	rō no
mute (adj)	口のきけない	kuchi no kike nai
deaf mute (adj)	ろうあの［聾唖の］	rōa no

mad, insane (adj)	狂気の	kyōki no
madman (demented person)	狂人	kyōjin
madwoman	狂女	kyōjo
to go insane	気が狂う	ki ga kurū

gene	遺伝子	idenshi
immunity	免疫	meneki
hereditary (adj)	遺伝性の	iden sei no
congenital (adj)	先天性の	senten sei no

virus	ウィルス	wirusu
microbe	細菌	saikin
bacterium	バクテリア	bakuteria
infection	伝染	densen

66. Symptoms. Treatments. Part 3

| hospital | 病院 | byōin |
| patient | 患者 | kanja |

diagnosis	診断	shindan
cure	療養	ryōyō
medical treatment	治療	chiryō
to get treatment	治療を受ける	chiryō wo ukeru
to treat (~ a patient)	治療する	chiryō suru
to nurse (look after)	看護する	kango suru
care (nursing ~)	看護	kango

operation, surgery	手術	shujutsu
to bandage (head, limb)	包帯をする	hōtai wo suru
bandaging	包帯を巻くこと	hōtai wo maku koto

vaccination	予防接種	yobō sesshu
to vaccinate (vt)	予防接種をする	yobō sesshu wo suru
injection, shot	注射	chūsha
to give an injection	注射する	chūsha suru
attack	発作	hossa

amputation	切断手術	setsudan shujutsu
to amputate (vt)	切断する	setsudan suru
coma	昏睡	konsui
to be in a coma	昏睡状態になる	konsui jōtai ni naru
intensive care	集中治療	shūchū chiryō
to recover (~ from flu)	回復する	kaifuku suru
condition (patient's ~)	体調	taichō
consciousness	意識	ishiki
memory (faculty)	記憶	kioku
to pull out (tooth)	抜く	nuku
filling	詰め物	tsume mono
to fill (a tooth)	詰め物をする	tsume mono wo suru
hypnosis	催眠術	saimin jutsu
to hypnotize (vt)	催眠術をかける	saimin jutsu wo kakeru

67. Medicine. Drugs. Accessories

medicine, drug	薬	kusuri
remedy	治療薬	chiryō yaku
to prescribe (vt)	処方する	shohō suru
prescription	処方	shohō
tablet, pill	錠剤	jōzai
ointment	軟膏	nankō
ampule	アンプル	anpuru
mixture	調合薬	chōgō yaku
syrup	シロップ	shiroppu
pill	丸剤	gan zai
powder	粉薬	konagusuri
gauze bandage	包帯	hōtai
cotton wool	脱脂綿	dasshimen
iodine	ヨード	yōdo
Band-Aid	ばんそうこう [絆創膏]	bansōkō
eyedropper	アイドロッパー	aidoroppā
thermometer	体温計	taionkei
syringe	注射器	chūsha ki
wheelchair	車椅子	kurumaisu
crutches	松葉杖	matsubazue
painkiller	痛み止め	itami tome
laxative	下剤	gezai
spirits (ethanol)	エタノール	etanoru
medicinal herbs	薬草	yakusō
herbal (~ tea)	薬草の	yakusō no

APARTMENT

T&P Books Publishing

68. Apartment

apartment	アパート	apāto
room	部屋	heya
bedroom	寝室	shinshitsu
dining room	食堂	shokudō
living room	居間	ima
study (home office)	書斎	shosai
entry room	玄関	genkan
bathroom (room with a bath or shower)	浴室	yokushitsu
half bath	トイレ	toire
ceiling	天井	tenjō
floor	床	yuka
corner	隅	sumi

69. Furniture. Interior

furniture	家具	kagu
table	テーブル	tēburu
chair	椅子	isu
bed	ベッド	beddo
couch, sofa	ソファ	sofa
armchair	肘掛け椅子	hijikake isu
bookcase	書棚	shodana
shelf	棚	tana
shelving unit	違い棚	chigaidana
wardrobe	ワードローブ	wādo rōbu
coat rack (wall-mounted ~)	ウォールハンガー	wōru hangā
coat stand	コートスタンド	kōto sutando
bureau, dresser	チェスト	chesuto
coffee table	コーヒーテーブル	kōhī tēburu
mirror	鏡	kagami
carpet	カーペット	kāpetto
rug, small carpet	マット	matto
fireplace	暖炉	danro
candle	ろうそく	rōsoku

candlestick	ろうそく立て	rōsoku date
drapes	カーテン	kāten
wallpaper	壁紙	kabegami
blinds (jalousie)	ブラインド	buraindo
table lamp	テーブルランプ	tēburu ranpu
wall lamp (sconce)	ウォールランプ	wōru ranpu
floor lamp	フロアスタンド	furoa sutando
chandelier	シャンデリア	shanderia
leg (of chair, table)	脚	ashi
armrest	肘掛け	hijikake
back (backrest)	背もたれ	semotare
drawer	引き出し	hikidashi

70. Bedding

bedclothes	寝具	shingu
pillow	枕	makura
pillowcase	枕カバー	makura kabā
duvet, comforter	毛布	mōfu
sheet	シーツ	shītsu
bedspread	ベッドカバー	beddo kabā

71. Kitchen

kitchen	台所	daidokoro
gas	ガス	gasu
gas stove (range)	ガスコンロ	gasu konro
electric stove	電気コンロ	denki konro
oven	オーブン	ōbun
microwave oven	電子レンジ	denshi renji
refrigerator	冷蔵庫	reizōko
freezer	冷凍庫	reitōko
dishwasher	食器洗い機	shokkiarai ki
meat grinder	肉挽き器	niku hiki ki
juicer	ジューサー	jūsā
toaster	トースター	tōsutā
mixer	ハンドミキサー	hando mikisā
coffee machine	コーヒーメーカー	kōhī mēkā
coffee pot	コーヒーポット	kōhī potto
coffee grinder	コーヒーグラインダー	kōhī guraindā
kettle	やかん	yakan
teapot	急須	kyūsu

lid	蓋 [ふた]	futa
tea strainer	茶漉し	chakoshi
spoon	さじ [匙]	saji
teaspoon	茶さじ	cha saji
soup spoon	大さじ [大匙]	ōsaji
fork	フォーク	fōku
knife	ナイフ	naifu
tableware (dishes)	食器	shokki
plate (dinner ~)	皿	sara
saucer	ソーサー	sōsā
shot glass	ショットグラス	shotto gurasu
glass (tumbler)	コップ	koppu
cup	カップ	kappu
sugar bowl	砂糖入れ	satō ire
salt shaker	塩入れ	shio ire
pepper shaker	胡椒入れ	koshō ire
butter dish	バター皿	batā zara
stock pot (soup pot)	両手鍋	ryō tenabe
frying pan (skillet)	フライパン	furaipan
ladle	おたま	o tama
colander	水切りボール	mizukiri bōru
tray (serving ~)	配膳盆	haizen bon
bottle	ボトル	botoru
jar (glass)	ジャー、瓶	jā, bin
can	缶	kan
bottle opener	栓抜き	sen nuki
can opener	缶切り	kankiri
corkscrew	コルク抜き	koruku nuki
filter	フィルター	firutā
to filter (vt)	フィルターにかける	firutā ni kakeru
trash, garbage (food waste, etc.)	ゴミ [ごみ]	gomi
trash can (kitchen ~)	ゴミ箱	gomibako

72. Bathroom

bathroom	浴室	yokushitsu
water	水	mizu
faucet	蛇口	jaguchi
hot water	温水	onsui
cold water	冷水	reisui
toothpaste	歯磨き粉	hamigakiko

| to brush one's teeth | 歯を磨く | ha wo migaku |
| toothbrush | 歯ブラシ | haburashi |

to shave (vi)	ひげを剃る	hige wo soru
shaving foam	シェービングフォーム	shēbingu fōmu
razor	剃刀	kamisori

to wash (one's hands, etc.)	洗う	arau
to take a bath	風呂に入る	furo ni hairu
shower	シャワー	shawā
to take a shower	シャワーを浴びる	shawā wo abiru

bathtub	浴槽	yokusō
toilet (toilet bowl)	トイレ、便器	toire, benki
sink (washbasin)	洗面台	senmen dai

| soap | 石鹸 | sekken |
| soap dish | 石鹸皿 | sekken zara |

sponge	スポンジ	suponji
shampoo	シャンプー	shanpū
towel	タオル	taoru
bathrobe	バスローブ	basurōbu

laundry (process)	洗濯	sentaku
washing machine	洗濯機	sentaku ki
to do the laundry	洗濯する	sentaku suru
laundry detergent	洗剤	senzai

73. Household appliances

TV set	テレビ	terebi
tape recorder	テープレコーダー	tēpurekōdā
VCR (video recorder)	ビデオ	bideo
radio	ラジオ	rajio
player (CD, MP3, etc.)	プレーヤー	purēyā

video projector	ビデオプロジェクター	bideo purojekutā
home movie theater	ホームシアター	hōmu shiatā
DVD player	DVDプレーヤー	dībuidī purēyā
amplifier	アンプ	anpu
video game console	ゲーム機	gēmu ki

video camera	ビデオカメラ	bideo kamera
camera (photo)	カメラ	kamera
digital camera	デジタルカメラ	dejitaru kamera

vacuum cleaner	掃除機	sōji ki
iron (e.g., steam ~)	アイロン	airon
ironing board	アイロン台	airondai

telephone	電話	denwa
mobile phone	携帯電話	keitai denwa
typewriter	タイプライター	taipuraitā
sewing machine	ミシン	mishin

microphone	マイクロフォン	maikurofon
headphones	ヘッドホン	heddohon
remote control (TV)	リモコン	rimokon

CD, compact disc	ＣＤ（シーディー）	shīdī
cassette	カセットテープ	kasettotēpu
vinyl record	レコード	rekōdo

T&P BOOKS

THE EARTH. WEATHER

T&P Books Publishing

space	宇宙	uchū
space (as adj)	宇宙の	uchū no
outer space	宇宙空間	uchū kūkan
world	世界	sekai
universe	宇宙	uchū
galaxy	銀河系	gingakei
star	星	hoshi
constellation	星座	seiza
planet	惑星	wakusei
satellite	衛星	eisei
meteorite	隕石	inseki
comet	彗星	suisei
asteroid	小惑星	shōwakusei
orbit	軌道	kidō
to revolve (~ around the Earth)	公転する	kōten suru
atmosphere	大気	taiki
the Sun	太陽	taiyō
solar system	太陽系	taiyōkei
solar eclipse	日食	nisshoku
the Earth	地球	chikyū
the Moon	月	tsuki
Mars	火星	kasei
Venus	金星	kinsei
Jupiter	木星	mokusei
Saturn	土星	dosei
Mercury	水星	suisei
Uranus	天王星	tennōsei
Neptune	海王星	kaiōsei
Pluto	冥王星	meiōsei
Milky Way	天の川	amanogawa
Great Bear (Ursa Major)	おおぐま座	ōguma za
North Star	北極星	hokkyokusei
Martian	火星人	kasei jin
extraterrestrial (n)	宇宙人	uchū jin

alien	異星人	i hoshi jin
flying saucer	空飛ぶ円盤	sora tobu enban
spaceship	宇宙船	uchūsen
space station	宇宙ステーション	uchū sutēshon
blast-off	打ち上げ	uchiage
engine	エンジン	enjin
nozzle	ノズル	nozuru
fuel	燃料	nenryō
cockpit, flight deck	コックピット	kokkupitto
antenna	アンテナ	antena
porthole	舷窓	gensō
solar panel	太陽電池	taiyō denchi
spacesuit	宇宙服	uchū fuku
weightlessness	無重力	mu jūryoku
oxygen	酸素	sanso
docking (in space)	ドッキング	dokkingu
to dock (vi, vt)	ドッキングする	dokkingu suru
observatory	天文台	tenmondai
telescope	望遠鏡	bōenkyō
to observe (vt)	観察する	kansatsu suru
to explore (vt)	探索する	tansaku suru

75. The Earth

the Earth	地球	chikyū
the globe (the Earth)	世界	sekai
planet	惑星	wakusei
atmosphere	大気	taiki
geography	地理学	chiri gaku
nature	自然	shizen
globe (table ~)	地球儀	chikyūgi
map	地図	chizu
atlas	地図帳	chizu chō
Europe	ヨーロッパ	yōroppa
Asia	アジア	ajia
Africa	アフリカ	afurika
Australia	オーストラリア	ōsutoraria
America	アメリカ	amerika
North America	北アメリカ	kita amerika
South America	南アメリカ	minami amerika

| Antarctica | 南極大陸 | nankyokutairiku |
| the Arctic | 北極 | hokkyoku |

76. Cardinal directions

north	北	kita
to the north	北へ	kita he
in the north	北に	kita ni
northern (adj)	北の	kita no

south	南	minami
to the south	南へ	minami he
in the south	南に	minami ni
southern (adj)	南の	minami no

west	西	nishi
to the west	西へ	nishi he
in the west	西に	nishi ni
western (adj)	西の	nishi no

east	東	higashi
to the east	東へ	higashi he
in the east	東に	higashi ni
eastern (adj)	東の	higashi no

77. Sea. Ocean

sea	海	umi
ocean	海洋	kaiyō
gulf (bay)	湾	wan
straits	海峡	kaikyō

land (solid ground)	乾燥地	kansō chi
continent (mainland)	大陸	tairiku
island	島	shima
peninsula	半島	hantō
archipelago	多島海	tatōkai

bay, cove	入り江	irie
harbor	泊地	hakuchi
lagoon	潟	kata
cape	岬	misaki

atoll	環礁	kanshō
reef	暗礁	anshō
coral	サンゴ	sango
coral reef	サンゴ礁	sangoshō
deep (adj)	深い	fukai

depth (deep water)	深さ	fuka sa
abyss	深淵	shinen
trench (e.g., Mariana ~)	海溝	kaikō
current (Ocean ~)	海流	kairyū
to surround (bathe)	取り囲む	torikakomu
shore	海岸	kaigan
coast	沿岸	engan
flow (flood tide)	満潮	manchō
ebb (ebb tide)	干潮	kanchō
shoal	砂州	sasu
bottom (~ of the sea)	底	soko
wave	波	nami
crest (~ of a wave)	波頭	namigashira
spume (sea foam)	泡	awa
storm (sea storm)	嵐	arashi
hurricane	ハリケーン	harikēn
tsunami	津波	tsunami
calm (dead ~)	凪	nagi
quiet, calm (adj)	穏やかな	odayaka na
pole	極地	kyokuchi
polar (adj)	極地の	kyokuchi no
latitude	緯度	ido
longitude	経度	keido
parallel	度線	dosen
equator	赤道	sekidō
sky	空	sora
horizon	地平線	chiheisen
air	空気	kūki
lighthouse	灯台	tōdai
to dive (vi)	飛び込む	tobikomu
to sink (ab. boat)	沈没する	chinbotsu suru
treasures	宝	takara

78. Seas' and Oceans' names

Atlantic Ocean	大西洋	taiseiyō
Indian Ocean	インド洋	indoyō
Pacific Ocean	太平洋	taiheiyō
Arctic Ocean	北氷洋	kitakōriyō
Black Sea	黒海	kokkai
Red Sea	紅海	kōkai

Yellow Sea	黄海	kōkai
White Sea	白海	hakkai
Caspian Sea	カスピ海	kasupikai
Dead Sea	死海	shikai
Mediterranean Sea	地中海	chichūkai
Aegean Sea	エーゲ海	ēgekai
Adriatic Sea	アドリア海	adoriakai
Arabian Sea	アラビア海	arabia kai
Sea of Japan	日本海	nihonkai
Bering Sea	ベーリング海	bēringukai
South China Sea	南シナ海	minami shinakai
Coral Sea	珊瑚海	sangokai
Tasman Sea	タスマン海	tasumankai
Caribbean Sea	カリブ海	karibukai
Barents Sea	バレンツ海	barentsukai
Kara Sea	カラ海	karakai
North Sea	北海	hokkai
Baltic Sea	バルト海	barutokai
Norwegian Sea	ノルウェー海	noruwē umi

79. Mountains

mountain	山	yama
mountain range	山脈	sanmyaku
mountain ridge	山稜	sanryō
summit, top	頂上	chōjō
peak	とがった山頂	togatta sanchō
foot (~ of the mountain)	麓	fumoto
slope (mountainside)	山腹	sanpuku
volcano	火山	kazan
active volcano	活火山	kakkazan
dormant volcano	休火山	kyūkazan
eruption	噴火	funka
crater	噴火口	funkakō
magma	岩漿、マグマ	ganshō, maguma
lava	溶岩	yōgan
molten (~ lava)	溶…	yō …
canyon	峡谷	kyōkoku
gorge	峡谷	kyōkoku
crevice	裂け目	sakeme

abyss (chasm)	奈落の底	naraku no soko
pass, col	峠	tōge
plateau	高原	kōgen
cliff	断崖	dangai
hill	丘	oka
glacier	氷河	hyōga
waterfall	滝	taki
geyser	間欠泉	kanketsusen
lake	湖	mizūmi
plain	平原	heigen
landscape	風景	fūkei
echo	こだま	kodama
alpinist	登山家	tozan ka
rock climber	ロッククライマー	rokku kuraimā
to conquer (in climbing)	征服する	seifuku suru
climb (an easy ~)	登山	tozan

80. Mountains names

The Alps	アルプス山脈	arupusu sanmyaku
Mont Blanc	モンブラン	monburan
The Pyrenees	ピレネー山脈	pirenē sanmyaku
The Carpathians	カルパティア山脈	karupatia sanmyaku
The Ural Mountains	ウラル山脈	uraru sanmyaku
The Caucasus Mountains	コーカサス山脈	kōkasasu sanmyaku
Mount Elbrus	エルブルス山	eruburusu san
The Altai Mountains	アルタイ山脈	arutai sanmyaku
The Tian Shan	天山山脈	amayama sanmyaku
The Pamir Mountains	パミール高原	pamīru kōgen
The Himalayas	ヒマラヤ	himaraya
Mount Everest	エベレスト	eberesuto
The Andes	アンデス山脈	andesu sanmyaku
Mount Kilimanjaro	キリマンジャロ	kirimanjaro

81. Rivers

river	川	kawa
spring (natural source)	泉	izumi
riverbed (river channel)	川床	kawadoko
basin	流域	ryūiki
to flow into ...	…に流れ込む	… ni nagarekomu
tributary	支流	shiryū

bank (of river)	川岸	kawagishi
current (stream)	流れ	nagare
downstream (adv)	下流の	karyū no
upstream (adv)	上流の	jōryū no
inundation	洪水	kōzui
flooding	氾濫	hanran
to overflow (vi)	氾濫する	hanran suru
to flood (vt)	水浸しにする	mizubitashi ni suru
shallow (shoal)	浅瀬	asase
rapids	急流	kyūryū
dam	ダム	damu
canal	運河	unga
reservoir (artificial lake)	ため池［溜池］	tameike
sluice, lock	水門	suimon
water body (pond, etc.)	水域	suīki
swamp (marshland)	沼地	numachi
bog, marsh	湿地	shicchi
whirlpool	渦	uzu
stream (brook)	小川	ogawa
drinking (ab. water)	飲用の	inyō no
fresh (~ water)	淡…	tan …
ice	氷	kōri
to freeze over (ab. river, etc.)	氷結する	hyōketsu suru

82. Rivers' names

Seine	セーヌ川	sēnu gawa
Loire	ロワール川	rowāru gawa
Thames	テムズ川	temuzu gawa
Rhine	ライン川	rain gawa
Danube	ドナウ川	donau gawa
Volga	ヴォルガ川	voruga gawa
Don	ドン川	don gawa
Lena	レナ川	rena gawa
Yellow River	黄河	kōga
Yangtze	長江	chōkō
Mekong	メコン川	mekon gawa
Ganges	ガンジス川	ganjisu gawa
Nile River	ナイル川	nairu gawa
Congo River	コンゴ川	kongo gawa

Okavango River	オカヴァンゴ川	okavango gawa
Zambezi River	ザンベジ川	zanbeji gawa
Limpopo River	リンポポ川	rinpopo gawa
Mississippi River	ミシシッピ川	mishishippi gawa

83. Forest

forest, wood	森林	shinrin
forest (as adj)	森林の	shinrin no
thick forest	密林	mitsurin
grove	木立	kodachi
forest clearing	空き地	akichi
thicket	やぶ ［藪］	yabu
scrubland	低木地域	teiboku chīki
footpath (troddenpath)	小道	komichi
gully	ガリ	gari
tree	木	ki
leaf	葉	ha
leaves (foliage)	葉っぱ	happa
fall of leaves	落葉	rakuyō
to fall (ab. leaves)	落ちる	ochiru
top (of the tree)	木のてっぺん	kinoteppen
branch	枝	eda
bough	主枝	shushi
bud (on shrub, tree)	芽 ［め］	me
needle (of pine tree)	松葉	matsuba
pine cone	松ぼっくり	matsubokkuri
hollow (in a tree)	樹洞	kihora
nest	巣	su
burrow (animal hole)	巣穴	su ana
trunk	幹	miki
root	根	ne
bark	樹皮	juhi
moss	コケ ［苔］	koke
to uproot (remove trees or tree stumps)	根こそぎにする	nekosogi ni suru
to chop down	切り倒す	kiritaosu
to deforest (vt)	切り払う	kiriharau
tree stump	切り株	kirikabu
campfire	焚火	takibi
forest fire	森林火災	shinrin kasai

to extinguish (vt)	火を消す	hi wo kesu
forest ranger	森林警備隊員	shinrin keibi taīn
protection	保護	hogo
to protect (~ nature)	保護する	hogo suru
poacher	密漁者	mitsuryō sha
steel trap	罠	wana
to pick (mushrooms)	摘み集める	tsumi atsumeru
to pick (berries)	採る	toru
to lose one's way	道に迷う	michi ni mayō

84. Natural resources

natural resources	天然資源	tennen shigen
minerals	鉱物資源	kōbutsu shigen
deposits	鉱床	kōshō
field (e.g., oilfield)	田	den
to mine (extract)	採掘する	saikutsu suru
mining (extraction)	採掘	saikutsu
ore	鉱石	kōseki
mine (e.g., for coal)	鉱山	kōzan
shaft (mine ~)	立坑	tatekō
miner	鉱山労働者	kōzan rōdō sha
gas (natural ~)	ガス	gasu
gas pipeline	ガスパイプライン	gasu paipurain
oil (petroleum)	石油	sekiyu
oil pipeline	石油パイプライン	sekiyu paipurain
oil well	油井	yusei
derrick (tower)	油井やぐら	yusei ya gura
tanker	タンカー	tankā
sand	砂	suna
limestone	石灰岩	sekkaigan
gravel	砂利	jari
peat	泥炭	deitan
clay	粘土	nendo
coal	石炭	sekitan
iron (ore)	鉄	tetsu
gold	金	kin
silver	銀	gin
nickel	ニッケル	nikkeru
copper	銅	dō
zinc	亜鉛	aen
manganese	マンガン	mangan
mercury	水銀	suigin

lead	鉛	namari
mineral	鉱物	kōbutsu
crystal	水晶	suishō
marble	大理石	dairiseki
uranium	ウラン	uran

85. Weather

weather	天気	tenki
weather forecast	天気予報	tenki yohō
temperature	温度	ondo
thermometer	温度計	ondo kei
barometer	気圧計	kiatsu kei

humid (adj)	湿度の	shitsudo no
humidity	湿度	shitsudo
heat (extreme ~)	猛暑	mōsho
hot (torrid)	暑い	atsui
it's hot	暑いです	atsui desu

| it's warm | 暖かいです | atatakai desu |
| warm (moderately hot) | 暖かい | atatakai |

| it's cold | 寒いです | samui desu |
| cold (adj) | 寒い | samui |

sun	太陽	taiyō
to shine (vi)	照る	teru
sunny (day)	晴れの	hare no
to come up (vi)	昇る	noboru
to set (vi)	沈む	shizumu

cloud	雲	kumo
cloudy (adj)	曇りの	kumori no
rain cloud	雨雲	amagumo
somber (gloomy)	どんよりした	donyori shi ta

rain	雨	ame
it's raining	雨が降っている	ame ga futte iru
rainy (~ day, weather)	雨の	ame no
to drizzle (vi)	そぼ降る	sobofuru

pouring rain	土砂降りの雨	doshaburi no ame
downpour	大雨	ōame
heavy (e.g., ~ rain)	激しい	hageshī
puddle	水溜り	mizutamari
to get wet (in rain)	ぬれる ［濡れる］	nureru

| fog (mist) | 霧 | kiri |
| foggy | 霧の | kiri no |

| snow | 雪 | yuki |
| it's snowing | 雪が降っている | yuki ga futte iru |

86. Severe weather. Natural disasters

thunderstorm	雷雨	raiu
lightning (~ strike)	稲妻	inazuma
to flash (vi)	ピカッと光る	pikatto hikaru

thunder	雷	kaminari
to thunder (vi)	雷が鳴る	kaminari ga naru
it's thundering	雷が鳴っている	kaminari ga natte iru

| hail | ひょう [雹] | hyō |
| it's hailing | ひょうが降っている | hyō ga futte iru |

| to flood (vt) | 水浸しにする | mizubitashi ni suru |
| flood, inundation | 洪水 | kōzui |

earthquake	地震	jishin
tremor, quake	震動	shindō
epicenter	震源地	shingen chi

| eruption | 噴火 | funka |
| lava | 溶岩 | yōgan |

twister	旋風	senpū
tornado	竜巻	tatsumaki
typhoon	台風	taifū

hurricane	ハリケーン	harikēn
storm	暴風	bōfū
tsunami	津波	tsunami

cyclone	サイクロン	saikuron
bad weather	悪い天気	warui tenki
fire (accident)	火事	kaji
disaster	災害	saigai
meteorite	隕石	inseki

avalanche	雪崩	nadare
snowslide	雪崩	nadare
blizzard	猛吹雪	mō fubuki
snowstorm	吹雪	fubuki

FAUNA

87. Mammals. Predators

predator	肉食獣	nikushoku juu
tiger	トラ［虎］	tora
lion	ライオン	raion
wolf	オオカミ	ōkami
fox	キツネ［狐］	kitsune
jaguar	ジャガー	jagā
leopard	ヒョウ［豹］	hyō
cheetah	チーター	chītā
black panther	黒豹	kuro hyō
puma	ピューマ	pyūma
snow leopard	雪豹	yuki hyō
lynx	オオヤマネコ	ōyamaneko
coyote	コヨーテ	koyōte
jackal	ジャッカル	jakkaru
hyena	ハイエナ	haiena

88. Wild animals

animal	動物	dōbutsu
beast (animal)	獣	shishi
squirrel	リス	risu
hedgehog	ハリネズミ［針鼠］	harinezumi
hare	ヘア	hea
rabbit	ウサギ［兎］	usagi
badger	アナグマ	anaguma
raccoon	アライグマ	araiguma
hamster	ハムスター	hamusutā
marmot	マーモット	māmotto
mole	モグラ	mogura
mouse	ネズミ	nezumi
rat	ラット	ratto
bat	コウモリ［蝙蝠］	kōmori
ermine	オコジョ	okojo
sable	クロテン	kuroten
marten	マツテン	matsu ten

| weasel | イタチ（鼬、鼬鼠） | itachi |
| mink | ミンク | minku |

| beaver | ビーバー | bībā |
| otter | カワウソ | kawauso |

horse	ウマ［馬］	uma
moose	ヘラジカ（箆鹿）	herajika
deer	シカ［鹿］	shika
camel	ラクダ［駱駝］	rakuda

bison	アメリカバイソン	amerika baison
aurochs	ヨーロッパバイソン	yōroppa baison
buffalo	水牛	suigyū

zebra	シマウマ［縞馬］	shimauma
antelope	レイヨウ	reiyō
roe deer	ノロジカ	noro jika
fallow deer	ダマジカ	damajika
chamois	シャモア	shamoa
wild boar	イノシシ［猪］	inoshishi

whale	クジラ［鯨］	kujira
seal	アザラシ	azarashi
walrus	セイウチ［海象］	seiuchi
fur seal	オットセイ［膃肭臍］	ottosei
dolphin	いるか［海豚］	iruka

bear	クマ［熊］	kuma
polar bear	ホッキョクグマ	hokkyokuguma
panda	パンダ	panda

monkey	サル［猿］	saru
chimpanzee	チンパンジー	chinpanjī
orangutan	オランウータン	oranwutan
gorilla	ゴリラ	gorira
macaque	マカク	makaku
gibbon	テナガザル	tenagazaru

| elephant | ゾウ［象］ | zō |
| rhinoceros | サイ［犀］ | sai |

| giraffe | キリン | kirin |
| hippopotamus | カバ［河馬］ | kaba |

| kangaroo | カンガルー | kangarū |
| koala (bear) | コアラ | koara |

mongoose	マングース	mangūsu
chinchilla	チンチラ	chinchira
skunk	スカンク	sukanku
porcupine	ヤマアラシ	yamārashi

89. Domestic animals

cat	猫	neko
tomcat	オス猫	osu neko
dog	犬	inu
horse	ウマ ［馬］	uma
stallion	種馬	taneuma
mare	雌馬	meuma
cow	雌牛	meushi
bull	雄牛	ōshi
ox	去勢牛	kyosei ushi
sheep (ewe)	羊	hitsuji
ram	雄羊	ohitsuji
goat	ヤギ ［山羊］	yagi
billy goat, he-goat	雄ヤギ	oyagi
donkey	ロバ	roba
mule	ラバ	raba
pig, hog	ブタ ［豚］	buta
piglet	子豚	kobuta
rabbit	カイウサギ ［飼兎］	kai usagi
hen (chicken)	ニワトリ ［鶏］	niwatori
rooster	おんどり ［雄鶏］	ondori
duck	アヒル	ahiru
drake	雄アヒル	oahiru
goose	ガチョウ	gachō
tom turkey, gobbler	雄七面鳥	oshichimenchō
turkey (hen)	七面鳥 ［シチメンチョウ］	shichimenchō
domestic animals	家畜	kachiku
tame (e.g., ~ hamster)	馴れた	nare ta
to tame (vt)	かいならす	kainarasu
to breed (vt)	飼養する	shiyō suru
farm	農場	nōjō
poultry	家禽	kakin
cattle	畜牛	chiku gyū
herd (cattle)	群れ	mure
stable	馬小屋	umagoya
pigsty	豚小屋	buta goya
cowshed	牛舎	gyūsha
rabbit hutch	ウサギ小屋	usagi koya
hen house	鶏小屋	niwatori goya

90. Birds

bird	鳥	tori
pigeon	鳩［ハト］	hato
sparrow	スズメ（雀）	suzume
tit	シジュウカラ［四十雀］	shijūkara
magpie	カササギ（鵲）	kasasagi

raven	ワタリガラス［渡鴉］	watari garasu
crow	カラス［鴉］	karasu
jackdaw	ニシコクマルガラス	nishikokumaru garasu
rook	ミヤマガラス［深山烏］	miyama garasu

duck	カモ［鴨］	kamo
goose	ガチョウ	gachō
pheasant	キジ	kiji

eagle	鷲	washi
hawk	鷹	taka
falcon	ハヤブサ［隼］	hayabusa
vulture	ハゲワシ	hagewashi
condor (Andean ~)	コンドル	kondoru

swan	白鳥［ハクチョウ］	hakuchō
crane	鶴［ツル］	tsuru
stork	シュバシコウ	shubashikō

parrot	オウム	ōmu
hummingbird	ハチドリ［蜂鳥］	hachidori
peacock	クジャク［孔雀］	kujaku

ostrich	ダチョウ［駝鳥］	dachō
heron	サギ［鷺］	sagi
flamingo	フラミンゴ	furamingo
pelican	ペリカン	perikan

| nightingale | サヨナキドリ | sayonakidori |
| swallow | ツバメ［燕］ | tsubame |

thrush	ノハラツグミ	nohara tsugumi
song thrush	ウタツグミ［歌鶫］	uta tsugumi
blackbird	クロウタドリ	kurōtadori

swift	アマツバメ［雨燕］	ama tsubame
lark	ヒバリ［雲雀］	hibari
quail	ウズラ	uzura

woodpecker	キツツキ	kitsutsuki
cuckoo	カッコウ［郭公］	kakkō
owl	トラフズク	torafuzuku
eagle owl	ワシミミズク	washi mimizuku

wood grouse	ヨーロッパオオライチョウ	yōroppa ōraichō
black grouse	クロライチョウ	kuro raichō
partridge	ヨーロッパヤマウズラ	yōroppa yamauzura
starling	ムクドリ	mukudori
canary	カナリア [金糸雀]	kanaria
hazel grouse	エゾライチョウ	ezo raichō
chaffinch	ズアオアトリ	zuaoatori
bullfinch	ウソ [鶯]	uso
seagull	カモメ [鷗]	kamome
albatross	アホウドリ	ahōdori
penguin	ペンギン	pengin

91. Fish. Marine animals

bream	ブリーム	burīmu
carp	コイ [鯉]	koi
perch	ヨーロピアンパーチ	yōropian pāchi
catfish	ナマズ	namazu
pike	カワカマス	kawakamasu
salmon	サケ	sake
sturgeon	チョウザメ [蝶鮫]	chōzame
herring	ニシン	nishin
Atlantic salmon	タイセイヨウサケ [大西洋鮭]	taiseiyō sake
mackerel	サバ [鯖]	saba
flatfish	カレイ [鰈]	karei
zander, pike perch	ザンダー	zandā
cod	タラ [鱈]	tara
tuna	マグロ [鮪]	maguro
trout	マス [鱒]	masu
eel	ウナギ [鰻]	unagi
electric ray	シビレエイ	shibireei
moray eel	ウツボ [鱓]	utsubo
piranha	ピラニア	pirania
shark	サメ [鮫]	same
dolphin	イルカ [海豚]	iruka
whale	クジラ [鯨]	kujira
crab	カニ [蟹]	kani
jellyfish	クラゲ [水母]	kurage
octopus	タコ [蛸]	tako
starfish	ヒトデ [海星]	hitode

| sea urchin | ウニ［海胆］ | uni |
| seahorse | タツノオトシゴ | tatsunootoshigo |

oyster	カキ［牡蠣］	kaki
shrimp	エビ	ebi
lobster	イセエビ	iseebi
spiny lobster	スパイニーロブスター	supainī robusutā

92. Amphibians. Reptiles

| snake | ヘビ（蛇） | hebi |
| venomous (snake) | 毒…、 有毒な | doku…, yūdoku na |

viper	クサリヘビ	kusarihebi
cobra	コブラ	kobura
python	ニシキヘビ	nishikihebi
boa	ボア	boa

grass snake	ヨーロッパヤマカガシ	yōroppa yamakagashi
rattle snake	ガラガラヘビ	garagarahebi
anaconda	アナコンダ	anakonda

lizard	トカゲ［蜥蜴］	tokage
iguana	イグアナ	iguana
monitor lizard	オオトカゲ	ōtokage
salamander	サンショウウオ［山椒魚］	sanshōuo
chameleon	カメレオン	kamereon
scorpion	サソリ［蠍］	sasori

turtle	カメ［亀］	kame
frog	蛙［カエル］	kaeru
toad	ヒキガエル	hikigaeru
crocodile	ワニ［鰐］	wani

93. Insects

insect, bug	昆虫	konchū
butterfly	チョウ［蝶］	chō
ant	アリ［蟻］	ari
fly	ハエ［蠅］	hae
mosquito	カ［蚊］	ka
beetle	甲虫	kabutomushi

wasp	ワスプ	wasupu
bee	ハチ［蜂］	hachi
bumblebee	マルハナバチ［丸花蜂］	maruhanabachi
gadfly	アブ［虻］	abu
spider	クモ［蜘蛛］	kumo

spider's web	クモの巣	kumo no su
dragonfly	トンボ［蜻蛉］	tonbo
grasshopper	キリギリス	kirigirisu
moth (night butterfly)	ガ［蛾］	ga
cockroach	ゴキブリ［蜚蠊］	gokiburi
tick	ダニ［蝨蟎、蜱］	dani
flea	ノミ［蚤］	nomi
midge	ヌカカ［糠蚊］	nukaka
locust	バッタ［飛蝗］	batta
snail	カタツムリ［蝸牛］	katatsumuri
cricket	コオロギ［蟋蟀、蛬］	kōrogi
lightning bug	ホタル［蛍、螢］	hotaru
ladybug	テントウムシ［天道虫］	tentōmushi
cockchafer	コフキコガネ	kofukikogane
leech	ヒル［蛭］	hiru
caterpillar	ケムシ［毛虫］	kemushi
earthworm	ミミズ［蚯蚓］	mimizu
larva	幼虫	yōchū

T&P BOOKS

FLORA

T&P Books Publishing

tree	木	ki
deciduous (adj)	落葉性の	rakuyō sei no
coniferous (adj)	針葉樹の	shinyōju no
evergreen (adj)	常緑の	jōryoku no
apple tree	りんごの木	ringonoki
pear tree	洋梨の木	yōnashinoki
sweet cherry tree	セイヨウミザクラ	seiyōmi zakura
sour cherry tree	スミミザクラ	sumimi zakura
plum tree	プラムトリー	puramu torī
birch	カバノキ	kabanoki
oak	オーク	ōku
linden tree	シナノキ［科の木］	shinanoki
aspen	ヤマナラシ［山鳴らし］	yamanarashi
maple	カエデ［楓］	kaede
spruce	スプルース	supurūsu
pine	マツ［松］	matsu
larch	カラマツ［唐松］	karamatsu
fir tree	モミ［樅］	momi
cedar	シダー	shidā
poplar	ポプラ	popura
rowan	ナナカマド	nanakamado
willow	ヤナギ［柳］	yanagi
alder	ハンノキ	hannoki
beech	ブナ	buna
elm	ニレ［楡］	nire
ash (tree)	トネリコ［梣］	toneriko
chestnut	クリ［栗］	kuri
magnolia	モクレン［木蓮］	mokuren
palm tree	ヤシ［椰子］	yashi
cypress	イトスギ［糸杉］	itosugi
mangrove	マングローブ	mangurōbu
baobab	バオバブ	baobabu
eucalyptus	ユーカリ	yūkari
sequoia	セコイア	sekoia

95. Shrubs

bush	低木	teiboku
shrub	潅木	kanboku
grapevine	ブドウ ［葡萄］	budō
vineyard	ブドウ園 ［葡萄園］	budōen
raspberry bush	ラズベリー	razuberī
blackcurrant bush	クロスグリ	kuro suguri
redcurrant bush	フサスグリ	fusa suguri
gooseberry bush	セイヨウスグリ	seiyō suguri
acacia	アカシア	akashia
barberry	メギ	megi
jasmine	ジャスミン	jasumin
juniper	セイヨウネズ	seiyōnezu
rosebush	バラの木	baranoki
dog rose	イヌバラ	inu bara

96. Fruits. Berries

fruit	果物	kudamono
fruits	果物	kudamono
apple	リンゴ	ringo
pear	洋梨	yōnashi
plum	プラム	puramu
strawberry	イチゴ（苺）	ichigo
cherry	チェリー	cherī
sour cherry	サワー チェリー	sawā cherī
sweet cherry	スイート チェリー	suīto cherī
grape	ブドウ ［葡萄］	budō
raspberry	ラズベリー（木苺）	razuberī
blackcurrant	クロスグリ	kuro suguri
redcurrant	フサスグリ	fusa suguri
gooseberry	セイヨウスグリ	seiyō suguri
cranberry	クランベリー	kuranberī
orange	オレンジ	orenji
mandarin	マンダリン	mandarin
pineapple	パイナップル	painappuru
banana	バナナ	banana
date	デーツ	dētsu
lemon	レモン	remon
apricot	アンズ ［杏子］	anzu

peach	モモ［桃］	momo
kiwi	キウイ	kiui
grapefruit	グレープフルーツ	gurēbu furūtsu
berry	ベリー	berī
berries	ベリー	berī
cowberry	コケモモ	kokemomo
field strawberry	ノイチゴ［野いちご］	noichigo
bilberry	ビルベリー	biruberī

97. Flowers. Plants

flower	花	hana
bouquet (of flowers)	花束	hanataba
rose (flower)	バラ	bara
tulip	チューリップ	chūrippu
carnation	カーネーション	kānēshon
gladiolus	グラジオラス	gurajiorasu
cornflower	ヤグルマギク［矢車菊］	yagurumagiku
bluebell	ホタルブクロ	hotarubukuro
dandelion	タンポポ［蒲公英］	tanpopo
camomile	カモミール	kamomīru
aloe	アロエ	aroe
cactus	サボテン	saboten
rubber plant, ficus	イチジク	ichijiku
lily	ユリ［百合］	yuri
geranium	ゼラニウム	zeranyūmu
hyacinth	ヒヤシンス	hiyashinsu
mimosa	ミモザ	mimoza
narcissus	スイセン［水仙］	suisen
nasturtium	キンレンカ［金蓮花］	kinrenka
orchid	ラン［蘭］	ran
peony	シャクヤク［芍薬］	shakuyaku
violet	スミレ［菫］	sumire
pansy	パンジー	panjī
forget-me-not	ワスレナグサ［勿忘草］	wasurenagusa
daisy	デイジー	deijī
poppy	ポピー	popī
hemp	アサ［麻］	asa
mint	ミント	minto
lily of the valley	スズラン［鈴蘭］	suzuran
snowdrop	スノードロップ	sunōdoroppu

nettle	イラクサ [刺草]	irakusa
sorrel	スイバ	suiba
water lily	スイレン [睡蓮]	suiren
fern	シダ	shida
lichen	地衣類	chī rui
greenhouse (tropical ~)	温室	onshitsu
lawn	芝生	shibafu
flowerbed	花壇	kadan
plant	植物	shokubutsu
grass	草	kusa
blade of grass	草の葉	kusa no ha
leaf	葉	ha
petal	花びら	hanabira
stem	茎	kuki
tuber	塊茎	kaikei
young plant (shoot)	シュート	shūto
thorn	茎針	kuki hari
to blossom (vi)	開花する	kaika suru
to fade, to wither	しおれる	shioreru
smell (odor)	香り	kaori
to cut (flowers)	切る	kiru
to pick (a flower)	摘む	tsumamu

98. Cereals, grains

grain	穀物	kokumotsu
cereal crops	禾穀類	kakokurui
ear (of barley, etc.)	花穂	kasui
wheat	コムギ [小麦]	komugi
rye	ライムギ [ライ麦]	raimugi
oats	オーツムギ [オーツ麦]	ōtsu mugi
millet	キビ [黍]	kibi
barley	オオムギ [大麦]	ōmugi
corn	トウモロコシ	tōmorokoshi
rice	イネ [稲]	ine
buckwheat	ソバ [蕎麦]	soba
pea plant	エンドウ [豌豆]	endō
kidney bean	インゲンマメ [隠元豆]	ingen mame
soy	ダイズ [大豆]	daizu
lentil	レンズマメ [レンズ豆]	renzu mame
beans (pulse crops)	豆類	mamerui

BOOKS

COUNTRIES OF
THE WORLD

T&P Books Publishing

Afghanistan	アフガニスタン	afuganisutan
Albania	アルバニア	arubania
Argentina	アルゼンチン	aruzenchin
Armenia	アルメニア	arumenia
Australia	オーストラリア	ōsutoraria
Austria	オーストリア	ōsutoria
Azerbaijan	アゼルバイジャン	azerubaijan
The Bahamas	バハマ	bahama
Bangladesh	バングラデシュ	banguradeshu
Belarus	ベラルーシー	berarūshī
Belgium	ベルギー	berugī
Bolivia	ボリビア	boribia
Bosnia and Herzegovina	ボスニア・ヘルツェゴヴィナ	bosunia herutsegovina
Brazil	ブラジル	burajiru
Bulgaria	ブルガリア	burugaria
Cambodia	カンボジア	kanbojia
Canada	カナダ	kanada
Chile	チリ	chiri
China	中国	chūgoku
Colombia	コロンビア	koronbia
Croatia	クロアチア	kuroachia
Cuba	キューバ	kyūba
Cyprus	キプロス	kipurosu
Czech Republic	チェコ	cheko
Denmark	デンマーク	denmāku
Dominican Republic	ドミニカ共和国	dominikakyōwakoku
Ecuador	エクアドル	ekuadoru
Egypt	エジプト	ejiputo
England	イギリス	igirisu
Estonia	エストニア	esutonia
Finland	フィンランド	finrando
France	フランス	furansu
French Polynesia	フランス領ポリネシア	furansu ryō porineshia
Georgia	グルジア	gurujia
Germany	ドイツ	doitsu
Ghana	ガーナ	gāna
Great Britain	グレートブリテン島	gurētoburiten tō
Greece	ギリシャ	girisha
Haiti	ハイチ	haichi
Hungary	ハンガリー	hangarī

100. Countries. Part 2

Iceland	アイスランド	aisurando
India	インド	indo
Indonesia	インドネシア	indoneshia
Iran	イラン	iran
Iraq	イラク	iraku
Ireland	アイルランド	airurando
Israel	イスラエル	isuraeru
Italy	イタリア	itaria
Jamaica	ジャマイカ	jamaika
Japan	日本	nihon
Jordan	ヨルダン	yorudan
Kazakhstan	カザフスタン	kazafusutan
Kenya	ケニア	kenia
Kirghizia	キルギス	kirugisu
Kuwait	クウェート	kuwēto
Laos	ラオス	raosu
Latvia	ラトビア	ratobia
Lebanon	レバノン	rebanon
Libya	リビア	ribia
Liechtenstein	リヒテンシュタイン	rihitenshutain
Lithuania	リトアニア	ritoania
Luxembourg	ルクセンブルク	rukusenburuku
Macedonia (Republic of ~)	マケドニア地方	makedonia chihō
Madagascar	マダガスカル	madagasukaru
Malaysia	マレーシア	marēshia
Malta	マルタ	maruta
Mexico	メキシコ	mekishiko
Moldova, Moldavia	モルドヴァ	morudova
Monaco	モナコ	monako
Mongolia	モンゴル	mongoru
Montenegro	モンテネグロ	monteneguro
Morocco	モロッコ	morokko
Myanmar	ミャンマー	myanmā
Namibia	ナミビア	namibia
Nepal	ネパール	nepāru
Netherlands	ネーデルラント	nēderuranto
New Zealand	ニュージーランド	nyūjīrando
North Korea	北朝鮮	kitachōsen
Norway	ノルウェー	noruwē

101. Countries. Part 3

Pakistan	パキスタン	pakisutan
Palestine	パレスチナ	paresuchina

Panama	パナマ	panama
Paraguay	パラグアイ	paraguai
Peru	ペルー	perū
Poland	ポーランド	pōrando
Portugal	ポルトガル	porutogaru
Romania	ルーマニア	rūmania
Russia	ロシア	roshia
Saudi Arabia	サウジアラビア	saujiarabia
Scotland	スコットランド	sukottorando
Senegal	セネガル	senegaru
Serbia	セルビア	serubia
Slovakia	スロバキア	surobakia
Slovenia	スロベニア	surobenia
South Africa	南アフリカ	minami afurika
South Korea	大韓民国	daikanminkoku
Spain	スペイン	supein
Suriname	スリナム	surinamu
Sweden	スウェーデン	suwēden
Switzerland	スイス	suisu
Syria	シリア	shiria
Taiwan	台湾	taiwan
Tajikistan	タジキスタン	tajikisutan
Tanzania	タンザニア	tanzania
Tasmania	タスマニア	tasumania
Thailand	タイ	tai
Tunisia	チュニジア	chunijia
Turkey	トルコ	toruko
Turkmenistan	トルクメニスタン	torukumenisutan
Ukraine	ウクライナ	ukuraina
United Arab Emirates	アラブ首長国連邦	arabu shuchō koku renpō
United States of America	アメリカ合衆国	amerika gasshūkoku
Uruguay	ウルグアイ	uruguai
Uzbekistan	ウズベキスタン	uzubekisutan
Vatican	バチカン	bachikan
Venezuela	ベネズエラ	benezuera
Vietnam	ベトナム	betonamu
Zanzibar	ザンジバル	zanjibaru

T&P BOOKS

GASTRONOMIC GLOSSARY

This section contains a lot of words and terms associated with food. This dictionary will make it easier for you to understand the menu at a restaurant and choose the right dish

T&P Books Publishing

English-Japanese gastronomic glossary

aftertaste	後味	atoaji
almond	アーモンド	āmondo
anise	アニス	anisu
aperitif	アペリティフ	aperitifu
appetite	食欲	shokuyoku
appetizer	前菜	zensai
apple	リンゴ	ringo
apricot	アンズ [杏子]	anzu
artichoke	アーティチョーク	ātichōku
asparagus	アスパラガス	asuparagasu
Atlantic salmon	タイセイヨウサケ [大西洋鮭]	taiseiyō sake
avocado	アボカド	abokado
bacon	ベーコン	bēkon
banana	バナナ	banana
barley	オオムギ [大麦]	ōmugi
bartender	バーテンダー	bātendā
basil	バジル	bajiru
bay leaf	ローリエ	rōrie
beans	豆類	mamerui
beef	牛肉	gyū niku
beer	ビール	bīru
beetroot	テーブルビート	tēburu bīto
bell pepper	コショウ	koshō
berries	ベリー	berī
berry	ベリー	berī
bilberry	ビルベリー	biruberī
birch bolete	ヤマイグチ	yamaiguchi
bitter	苦い	nigai
black coffee	ブラックコーヒー	burakku kōhī
black pepper	黒コショウ	kuro koshō
black tea	紅茶	kō cha
blackberry	ブラックベリー	burakku berī
blackcurrant	クロスグリ	kuro suguri
boiled	煮た	ni ta
bottle opener	栓抜き	sen nuki
bread	パン	pan
breakfast	朝食	chōshoku
bream	ブリーム	burīmu
broccoli	ブロッコリー	burokkorī
Brussels sprouts	メキャベツ	mekyabetsu
buckwheat	ソバ [蕎麦]	soba
butter	バター	batā
buttercream	バタークリーム	batā kurīmu

cabbage	キャベツ	kyabetsu
cake	ケーキ	kēki
cake	ケーキ	kēki
calorie	カロリー	karorī
can opener	缶切り	kankiri
candy	キャンディー	kyandī
canned food	缶詰	kanzume
cappuccino	カプチーノ	kapuchīno
caraway	キャラウェイ	kyarawei
carbohydrates	炭水化物	tansuikabutsu
carbonated	炭酸の	tansan no
carp	コイ［鯉］	koi
carrot	ニンジン［人参］	ninjin
catfish	ナマズ	namazu
cauliflower	カリフラワー	karifurawā
caviar	キャビア	kyabia
celery	セロリ	serori
cep	ヤマドリタケ	yamadori take
cereal crops	禾穀類	kakokurui
cereal grains	穀物	kokumotsu
champagne	シャンパン	shanpan
chanterelle	アンズタケ［杏茸］	anzu take
check	お勘定	okanjō
cheese	チーズ	chīzu
chewing gum	チューインガム	chūin gamu
chicken	鶏	niwatori
chocolate	チョコレート	chokorēto
chocolate	チョコレートの	chokorēto no
cinnamon	シナモン	shinamon
clear soup	ブイヨン	buiyon
cloves	クローブ	kurōbu
cocktail	カクテル	kakuteru
coconut	ココナッツ	koko nattsu
cod	タラ［鱈］	tara
coffee	コーヒー	kōhī
coffee with milk	ミルク入りコーヒー	miruku iri kōhī
cognac	コニャック	konyakku
cold	冷たい	tsumetai
condensed milk	練乳	rennyū
condiment	調味料	chōmiryō
confectionery	菓子類	kashi rui
cookies	クッキー	kukkī
coriander	コリアンダー	koriandā
corkscrew	コルク抜き	koruku nuki
corn	トウモロコシ	tōmorokoshi
corn	トウモロコシ	tōmorokoshi
cornflakes	コーンフレーク	kōn furēku
course, dish	料理	ryōri
cowberry	コケモモ	kokemomo
crab	カニ［蟹］	kani
cranberry	クランベリー	kuranberī
cream	クリーム	kurīmu

crumb	くず	kuzu
cucumber	きゅうり［胡瓜］	kyūri
cuisine	料理	ryōri
cup	カップ	kappu
dark beer	黒ビール	kuro bīru
date	デーツ	dētsu
death cap	タマゴテングタケ ［卵天狗茸］	tamagotengu take
dessert	デザート	dezāto
diet	ダイエット	daietto
dill	ディル	diru
dinner	夕食	yūshoku
dried	干した	hoshi ta
drinking water	飲用水	inyō sui
duck	ダック	dakku
ear	花穂	kasui
edible mushroom	食用キノコ	shokuyō kinoko
eel	ウナギ［鰻］	unagi
egg	卵	tamago
egg white	卵の白身	tamago no shiromi
egg yolk	卵の黄身	tamago no kimi
eggplant	ナス	nasu
eggs	卵	tamago
Enjoy your meal!	どうぞお召し上がり 下さい！	dōzo o meshiagarikudasai!
fats	脂肪	shibō
field strawberry	ノイチゴ［野いちご］	noichigo
fig	イチジク	ichijiku
filling	フィリング	firingu
fish	魚	sakana
flatfish	カレイ［鰈］	karei
flour	小麦粉	komugiko
fly agaric	ベニテングタケ ［紅天狗茸］	benitengu take
food	食べ物	tabemono
fork	フォーク	fōku
freshly squeezed juice	搾りたてのジュース	shibori tate no jūsu
fried	揚げた	age ta
fried eggs	目玉焼き	medamayaki
fried meatballs	クロケット	kuroketto
frozen	冷凍の	reitō no
fruit	果物	kudamono
fruits	果物	kudamono
game	獲物	emono
gammon	ガモン	gamon
garlic	ニンニク	ninniku
gin	ジン	jin
ginger	生姜、ジンジャー	shōga, jinjā
glass	ガラスのコップ	garasu no koppu
glass	ワイングラス	wain gurasu
goose	ガチョウ	gachō
gooseberry	セイヨウスグリ	seiyō suguri

grain	穀物	kokumotsu
grape	ブドウ［葡萄］	budō
grapefruit	グレープフルーツ	gurēbu furūtsu
green tea	緑茶	ryoku cha
greens	青物	aomono
halibut	ハリバット	haribatto
ham	ハム	hamu
hamburger	挽肉	hikiniku
hamburger	ハンバーガー	hanbāgā
hazelnut	ヘーゼルナッツ	hēzeru nattsu
herring	ニシン	nishin
honey	蜂蜜	hachimitsu
horseradish	セイヨウワサビ	seiyō wasabi
hot	熱い	atsui
ice	水	kōri
ice-cream	アイスクリーム	aisukurīmu
instant coffee	インスタントコーヒー	insutanto kōhī
jam	ジャム	jamu
jam	ジャム	jamu
juice	ジュース	jūsu
kidney bean	金時豆	kintoki mame
kiwi	キウイ	kiui
knife	ナイフ	naifu
lamb	子羊肉	kohitsuji niku
lard	ラード	rādo
lemon	レモン	remon
lemonade	レモネード	remonēdo
lentil	レンズマメ［レンズ豆］	renzu mame
lettuce	レタス	retasu
light beer	ライトビール	raito bīru
liqueur	リキュール	rikyūru
liquors	アルコール	arukōru
liver	レバー	rebā
lunch	昼食	chūshoku
mackerel	サバ［鯖］	saba
mandarin	マンダリン	mandarin
mango	マンゴー	mangō
margarine	マーガリン	māgarin
marmalade	マーマレード	māmarēdo
mashed potatoes	マッシュポテト	masshupoteto
mayonnaise	マヨネーズ	mayonēzu
meat	肉	niku
melon	メロン	meron
menu	メニュー	menyū
milk	乳、ミルク	nyū, miruku
milkshake	ミルクセーキ	miruku sēki
millet	キビ［黍］	kibi
mineral water	ミネラルウォーター	mineraru wōtā
morel	アミガサタケ［網笠茸］	amigasa take
mushroom	キノコ［茸］	kinoko
mustard	マスタード	masutādo
non-alcoholic	ノンアルコールの	non arukŌru no

noodles	麺	men
oats	オーツムギ［オーツ麦］	ōtsu mugi
olive oil	オリーブ油	orĩbu yu
olives	オリーブ	orĩbu
omelet	オムレツ	omuretsu
onion	たまねぎ［玉葱］	tamanegi
orange	オレンジ	orenji
orange juice	オレンジジュース	orenji jūsu
orange-cap boletus	アカエノキンチャ ヤマイグチ	akaenokincha yamaiguchi
oyster	カキ［牡蠣］	kaki
pâté	パテ	pate
papaya	パパイヤ	papaiya
paprika	パプリカ	papurika
parsley	パセリ	paseri
pasta	パスタ	pasuta
pea	エンドウ	endō
peach	モモ［桃］	momo
peanut	ピーナッツ	pĩnattsu
pear	洋梨	yōnashi
peel	皮	kawa
perch	ヨーロピアンパーチ	yōropian pāchi
pickled	酢漬けの	suzuke no
pie	パイ	pai
piece	一切れ	ichi kire
pike	カワカマス	kawakamasu
pike perch	ザンダー	zandā
pineapple	パイナップル	painappuru
pistachios	ピスタチオ	pisutachio
pizza	ピザ	piza
plate	皿	sara
plum	プラム	puramu
poisonous mushroom	毒キノコ	doku kinoko
pomegranate	ザクロ	zakuro
pork	豚肉	buta niku
porridge	ポリッジ	porijji
portion	一人前	ichi ninmae
potato	ジャガイモ	jagaimo
proteins	タンパク質［蛋白質］	tanpaku shitsu
pub, bar	パブ、バー	pabu, bā
pudding	プディング	pudingu
pumpkin	カボチャ	kabocha
rabbit	兎肉	usagi niku
radish	ハツカダイコン	hatsukadaikon
raisin	レーズン	rēzun
raspberry	ラズベリー（木苺）	razuberĩ
recipe	レシピ	reshipi
red pepper	赤唐辛子	aka tōgarashi
red wine	赤ワイン	aka wain
redcurrant	フサスグリ	fusa suguri
refreshing drink	清涼飲料水	seiryõinryõsui
rice	米	kome

rum	ラム酒	ramu shu
russula	ベニタケ［紅茸］	beni take
rye	ライムギ［ライ麦］	raimugi
saffron	サフラン	safuran
salad	サラダ	sarada
salmon	サケ［鮭］	sake
salt	塩	shio
salty	塩味の	shioaji no
sandwich	サンドイッチ	sandoicchi
sardine	イワシ	iwashi
sauce	ソース	sōsu
saucer	ソーサー	sōsā
sausage	ソーセージ	sōsēji
seafood	魚介	gyokai
sesame	ゴマ［胡麻］	goma
shark	サメ［鮫］	same
shrimp	エビ	ebi
side dish	付け合わせ	tsukeawase
slice	スライス	suraisu
smoked	薫製の	kunsei no
soft drink	炭酸飲料	tansan inryō
soup	スープ	sūpu
soup spoon	大さじ［大匙］	ōsaji
sour cherry	サワー チェリー	sawā cherī
sour cream	サワークリーム	sawā kurīmu
soy	ダイズ［大豆］	daizu
spaghetti	スパゲッティ	supagetti
sparkling	発泡性の	happō sei no
spice	香辛料	kōshinryō
spinach	ホウレンソウ	hōrensō
spiny lobster	伊勢エビ	ise ebi
spoon	スプーン	supūn
squid	イカ	ika
steak	ビーフステーキ	bīfusutēki
stew	シチュー	shichū
still	無炭酸の	mu tansan no
strawberry	イチゴ（苺）	ichigo
sturgeon	チョウザメ	chōzame
sugar	砂糖	satō
sunflower oil	ひまわり油	himawari yu
sweet	甘い	amai
sweet cherry	スイート チェリー	suīto cherī
taste, flavor	味	aji
tasty	美味しい	oishī
tea	茶	cha
teaspoon	茶さじ	cha saji
tip	チップ	chippu
tomato	トマト	tomato
tomato juice	トマトジュース	tomato jūsu
tongue	タン	tan
toothpick	つまようじ［爪楊枝］	tsumayōji
trout	マス［鱒］	masu

tuna	マグロ［鮪］	maguro
turkey	七面鳥	shichimenchuō
turnip	カブ	kabu
veal	子牛肉	kōshi niku
vegetable oil	植物油	shokubutsu yu
vegetables	野菜	yasai
vegetarian	ベジタリアン	bejitarian
vegetarian	ベジタリアン用の	bejitarian yōno
vermouth	ベルモット	berumotto
vienna sausage	ソーセージ	sōsēji
vinegar	酢、ビネガー	su, binegā
vitamin	ビタミン	bitamin
vodka	ウォッカ	wokka
waffles	ワッフル	waffuru
waiter	ウェイター	weitā
waitress	ウェートレス	wētoresu
walnut	クルミ（胡桃）	kurumi
water	水	mizu
watermelon	スイカ	suika
wheat	コムギ［小麦］	komugi
whisky	ウイスキー	uisukī
white wine	白ワイン	shiro wain
wine	ワイン	wain
wine list	ワインリスト	wain risuto
with ice	氷入りの	kōri iri no
yogurt	ヨーグルト	yōguruto
zucchini	ズッキーニ	zukkīni

Japanese-English gastronomic glossary

アーモンド	āmondo	almond
アーティチョーク	ātichōku	artichoke
アボカド	abokado	avocado
揚げた	age ta	fried
味	aji	taste, flavor
アイスクリーム	aisukurīmu	ice-cream
赤ワイン	aka wain	red wine
赤唐辛子	aka tōgarashi	red pepper
アカエノキンチャヤマイグチ	akaenokincha yamaiguchi	orange-cap boletus
甘い	amai	sweet
アミガサタケ [網笠茸]	amigasa take	morel
アンズ [杏子]	anzu	apricot
アンズタケ [杏茸]	anzu take	chanterelle
アニス	anisu	anise
青物	aomono	greens
アペリティフ	aperitifu	aperitif
アルコール	arukōru	liquors
アスパラガス	asuparagasu	asparagus
後味	atoaji	aftertaste
熱い	atsui	hot
バーテンダー	bātendā	bartender
バジル	bajiru	basil
バナナ	banana	banana
バター	batā	butter
バタークリーム	batā kurīmu	buttercream
ビール	bīru	beer
ビーフステーキ	bīfusutēki	steak
ビルベリー	biruberī	bilberry
ビタミン	bitamin	vitamin
ブドウ [葡萄]	budō	grape
ブイヨン	buiyon	clear soup
ブラックベリー	burakku berī	blackberry
ブラックコーヒー	burakku kōhī	black coffee
ブリーム	burīmu	bream
ブロッコリー	burokkorī	broccoli
豚肉	buta niku	pork
ベーコン	bēkon	bacon
ベジタリアン	bejitarian	vegetarian
ベジタリアン用の	bejitarian yōno	vegetarian
ベニタケ [紅茸]	beni take	russula
ベニテングタケ [紅天狗茸]	benitengu take	fly agaric
ベリー	berī	berry

ベリー	berī	berries
ベルモット	berumotto	vermouth
ワイン	wain	wine
ワイングラス	wain gurasu	glass
ワインリスト	wain risuto	wine list
ワッフル	waffuru	waffles
ウェイター	weitā	waiter
ウォッカ	wokka	vodka
ウェートレス	wētoresu	waitress
ガモン	gamon	gammon
ガラスのコップ	garasu no koppu	glass
ガチョウ	gachō	goose
魚介	gyokai	seafood
ゴマ［胡麻］	goma	sesame
グレープフルーツ	gurēbu furūtsu	grapefruit
牛肉	gyū niku	beef
ダイズ［大豆］	daizu	soy
ダイエット	daietto	diet
ダック	dakku	duck
ザクロ	zakuro	pomegranate
ザンダー	zandā	pike perch
ズッキーニ	zukkīni	zucchini
前菜	zensai	appetizer
ディル	diru	dill
どうぞお召し上がり下さい！	dōzo o meshiagarikudasai!	Enjoy your meal!
毒キノコ	doku kinoko	poisonous mushroom
デーツ	dētsu	date
デザート	dezāto	dessert
エンドウ	endō	pea
ヨーグルト	yōguruto	yogurt
洋梨	yōnashi	pear
ヨーロピアンパーチ	yōropian pāchi	perch
ジャガイモ	jagaimo	potato
ジャム	jamu	jam
ジャム	jamu	jam
ジン	jin	gin
ジュース	jūsu	juice
イワシ	iwashi	sardine
イカ	ika	squid
飲用水	inyō sui	drinking water
インスタントコーヒー	insutanto kōhī	instant coffee
伊勢エビ	ise ebi	spiny lobster
一切れ	ichi kire	piece
一人前	ichi ninmae	portion
イチゴ（苺）	ichigo	strawberry
イチジク	ichijiku	fig
カボチャ	kabocha	pumpkin
カブ	kabu	turnip
皮	kawa	peel
カワカマス	kawakamasu	pike
カキ［牡蠣］	kaki	oyster

禾穀類	kakokurui	cereal crops
カクテル	kakuteru	cocktail
缶詰	kanzume	canned food
カニ [蟹]	kani	crab
缶切り	kankiri	can opener
カップ	kappu	cup
カプチーノ	kapuchīno	cappuccino
カリフラワー	karifurawā	cauliflower
カロリー	karorī	calorie
カレイ [鰈]	karei	flatfish
花穂	kasui	ear
菓子類	kashi rui	confectionery
キビ [黍]	kibi	millet
キノコ [茸]	kinoko	mushroom
金時豆	kintoki mame	kidney bean
キウイ	kiui	kiwi
紅茶	kō cha	black tea
コーンフレーク	kōn furēku	cornflakes
氷	kōri	ice
氷入りの	kōri iri no	with ice
コーヒー	kōhī	coffee
子牛肉	kōshi niku	veal
香辛料	kōshinryō	spice
コイ [鯉]	koi	carp
ココナッツ	koko nattsu	coconut
穀物	kokumotsu	cereal grains
穀物	kokumotsu	grain
コケモモ	kokemomo	cowberry
コムギ [小麦]	komugi	wheat
小麦粉	komugiko	flour
米	kome	rice
コニャック	konyakku	cognac
コリアンダー	koriandā	coriander
コルク抜き	koruku nuki	corkscrew
子羊肉	kohitsuji niku	lamb
コショウ	koshō	bell pepper
果物	kudamono	fruit
果物	kudamono	fruits
くず	kuzu	crumb
クッキー	kukkī	cookies
薫製の	kunsei no	smoked
クランベリー	kuranberī	cranberry
クリーム	kurīmu	cream
黒ビール	kuro bīru	dark beer
黒コショウ	kuro koshō	black pepper
クロスグリ	kuro suguri	blackcurrant
クローブ	kurōbu	cloves
クロケット	kuroketto	fried meatballs
クルミ（胡桃）	kurumi	walnut
ケーキ	kēki	cake
ケーキ	kēki	cake
きゅうり [胡瓜]	kyūri	cucumber

キャビア	kyabia	caviar
キャベツ	kyabetsu	cabbage
キャンディー	kyandī	candy
キャラウェイ	kyarawei	caraway
マーガリン	māgarin	margarine
マーマレード	māmarēdo	marmalade
マグロ [鮪]	maguro	tuna
マヨネーズ	mayonēzu	mayonnaise
豆類	mamerui	beans
マンゴー	mangō	mango
マンダリン	mandarin	mandarin
マス [鱒]	masu	trout
マスタード	masutādo	mustard
マッシュポテト	masshupoteto	mashed potatoes
水	mizu	water
ミネラルウォーター	mineraru wōtā	mineral water
ミルク入りコーヒー	miruku iri kōhī	coffee with milk
ミルクセーキ	miruku sēki	milkshake
モモ [桃]	momo	peach
無炭酸の	mu tansan no	still
目玉焼き	medamayaki	fried eggs
メキャベツ	mekyabetsu	Brussels sprouts
麺	men	noodles
メニュー	menyū	menu
メロン	meron	melon
ナイフ	naifu	knife
ナマズ	namazu	catfish
ナス	nasu	eggplant
煮た	ni ta	boiled
鶏	niwatori	chicken
苦い	nigai	bitter
肉	niku	meat
ニンジン [人参]	ninjin	carrot
ニンニク	ninniku	garlic
ニシン	nishin	herring
ノイチゴ [野いちご]	noichigo	field strawberry
ノンアルコールの	non arukŌru no	non-alcoholic
乳、ミルク	nyū, miruku	milk
オオムギ [大麦]	ōmugi	barley
大さじ [大匙]	ōsaji	soup spoon
オーツムギ [オーツ麦]	ōtsu mugi	oats
美味しい	oishī	tasty
お勘定	okanjō	check
オムレツ	omuretsu	omelet
オリーブ	orību	olives
オリーブ油	orību yu	olive oil
オレンジ	orenji	orange
オレンジジュース	orenji jūsu	orange juice
パブ、バー	pabu, bā	pub, bar
パイナップル	painappuru	pineapple
パイ	pai	pie
パン	pan	bread

パパイヤ	papaiya	papaya
パプリカ	papurika	paprika
パスタ	pasuta	pasta
パセリ	paseri	parsley
パテ	pate	pâté
ピーナッツ	pīnattsu	peanut
ピザ	piza	pizza
ピスタチオ	pisutachio	pistachios
ポリッジ	porijji	porridge
プディング	pudingu	pudding
プラム	puramu	plum
ラード	rādo	lard
ラズベリー（木苺）	razuberī	raspberry
ライムギ［ライ麦］	raimugi	rye
ライトビール	raito bīru	light beer
ラム酒	ramu shu	rum
料理	ryōri	course, dish
料理	ryōri	cuisine
緑茶	ryoku cha	green tea
リキュール	rikyūru	liqueur
リンゴ	ringo	apple
ローリエ	rōrie	bay leaf
レーズン	rēzun	raisin
レバー	rebā	liver
冷凍の	reitō no	frozen
レモン	remon	lemon
レモネード	remonēdo	lemonade
レンズマメ［レンズ豆］	renzu mame	lentil
練乳	rennyū	condensed milk
レタス	retasu	lettuce
レシピ	reshipi	recipe
サバ［鯖］	saba	mackerel
サワークリーム	sawā kurīmu	sour cream
サワー チェリー	sawā cherī	sour cherry
魚	sakana	fish
サケ［鮭］	sake	salmon
サメ［鮫］	same	shark
サンドイッチ	sandoicchi	sandwich
皿	sara	plate
サラダ	sarada	salad
砂糖	satō	sugar
サフラン	safuran	saffron
ソーサー	sōsā	saucer
ソース	sōsu	sauce
ソーセージ	sōsēji	sausage
ソーセージ	sōsēji	vienna sausage
ソバ［蕎麦］	soba	buckwheat
酢、ビネガー	su, binegā	vinegar
スープ	sūpu	soup
酢漬けの	suzuke no	pickled
スイート チェリー	suīto cherī	sweet cherry
スイカ	suika	watermelon

スパゲッティ	supagetti	spaghetti
スプーン	supūn	spoon
スライス	suraisu	slice
セイヨウワサビ	seiyō wasabi	horseradish
セイヨウスグリ	seiyō suguri	gooseberry
清涼飲料水	seiryōinryōsui	refreshing drink
栓抜き	sen nuki	bottle opener
セロリ	serori	celery
食べ物	tabemono	food
タイセイヨウサケ [大西洋鮭]	taiseiyō sake	Atlantic salmon
卵	tamago	egg
卵	tamago	eggs
卵の黄身	tamago no kimi	egg yolk
卵の白身	tamago no shiromi	egg white
タマゴテングタケ [卵天狗茸]	tamagotengu take	death cap
たまねぎ [玉葱]	tamanegi	onion
タン	tan	tongue
タンパク質 [蛋白質]	tanpaku shitsu	proteins
炭酸飲料	tansan inryō	soft drink
炭酸の	tansan no	carbonated
炭水化物	tansuikabutsu	carbohydrates
タラ [鱈]	tara	cod
トウモロコシ	tōmorokoshi	corn
トウモロコシ	tōmorokoshi	corn
トマト	tomato	tomato
トマトジュース	tomato jūsu	tomato juice
テーブルビート	tēburu bīto	beetroot
ウイスキー	uisukī	whisky
ウナギ [鰻]	unagi	eel
兎肉	usagi niku	rabbit
フィリング	firingu	filling
フォーク	fōku	fork
フサスグリ	fusa suguri	redcurrant
ハム	hamu	ham
ハンバーガー	hanbāgā	hamburger
発泡性の	happō sei no	sparkling
ハリバット	haribatto	halibut
ハツカダイコン	hatsukadaikon	radish
蜂蜜	hachimitsu	honey
挽肉	hikiniku	hamburger
ひまわり油	himawari yu	sunflower oil
ホウレンソウ	hōrensō	spinach
干した	hoshi ta	dried
ヘーゼルナッツ	hēzeru nattsu	hazelnut
付け合わせ	tsukeawase	side dish
つまようじ [爪楊枝]	tsumayōji	toothpick
冷たい	tsumetai	cold
茶	cha	tea
茶さじ	cha saji	teaspoon
チーズ	chīzu	cheese

チップ	chippu	tip
チョウザメ	chōzame	sturgeon
調味料	chōmiryō	condiment
朝食	chōshoku	breakfast
チョコレート	chokorēto	chocolate
チョコレートの	chokorēto no	chocolate
チューインガム	chūin gamu	chewing gum
昼食	chūshoku	lunch
シャンパン	shanpan	champagne
脂肪	shibō	fats
搾りたてのジュース	shibori tate no jūsu	freshly squeezed juice
シナモン	shinamon	cinnamon
塩	shio	salt
塩味の	shioaji no	salty
白ワイン	shiro wain	white wine
七面鳥	shichimenchuō	turkey
シチュー	shichū	stew
生姜、ジンジャー	shōga, jinjā	ginger
植物油	shokubutsu yu	vegetable oil
食用キノコ	shokuyō kinoko	edible mushroom
食欲	shokuyoku	appetite
エビ	ebi	shrimp
獲物	emono	game
夕食	yūshoku	dinner
ヤマドリタケ	yamadori take	cep
ヤマイグチ	yamaiguchi	birch bolete
野菜	yasai	vegetables